The Leprechaun Companion

Little cow-boy, what have you heard,
Up on the lovely rath's green mound?
Only the plaintive yellow bird
Sighing in sultry fields around,
Chary, chary, chary, chee-ee!
Only the grasshopper and the bee? -
Tip-tap, rip-rap,
Tick-a-tack-too!
Scarlet leather, sewn together,
This will make a shoe.
Left, right, pull it tight;
Summer days are warm;
Underground in winter,
Laughing at the storm!'
Lay your ear close to the hill.
Do you not catch the tiny clamour,
Busy click of an elfin hammer,
Voice of the leprechaun singing shrill
As he merrily plies his trade?
He's a span and a quarter in height.
Get him and hold him tight,
And you're a made Man!

1

the Leprechaun Companion

Niall Macnamara

Illustrated by Wayne Anderson

PAVILION

Dedicated to Eunice McMullen
Vivienne and Lorna Hughes

First published in Great Britain in 1999 by
PAVILION BOOKS LIMITED
London House, Great Eastern Wharf
Parkgate Road, London SW11 4NQ

Text © Nigel Suckling
Illustrations © Wayne Anderson

The moral right of the author and illustrator
has been asserted

Art Direction and design by David Costa and Fiona Andreanelli at Wherefore Art?

A CIP catalogue record for this book is available
from the British Library.

ISBN 1 86205 193 3

Set in Pinnacle & Angelo
Printed in Singapore by Imago

2 4 6 8 10 9 7 5 3 1

This book can be ordered direct from the publisher. Please contact
the Marketing Department. But try your bookshop first.

Contents

INTRODUCTION

ANY PEOPLE BELIEVE
leprechauns are simply a
dwindled folk memory of the
tall and graceful *Tuatha de Danann*, an elvish folk said
to have ruled Ireland by magic in ancient times, before
the arrival of the Sons of Mil. This is not so.
Leprechauns are a separate race, almost as ancient and
as proud in their own way as the *Tuatha*, and they
take great offence at being mistaken for anything
other than what they are.

Others say leprechauns are just a load of old
cobblers. Which is true of course because a thousand
years is a sprightly age for a leprechaun, and they are
famous for their shoemaking; but they have many
other talents besides. They are also great tinkers
(partly because in the old days their shoes were made
of metal) and have proved themselves perfectly equal
to much modern technology. Many a tractor in the
west of Ireland owes its survival more to the tinkering
of leprechauns than the care of the local garage,
which it will not have seen for years.

Leprechauns are generally classed among the solitary
faeries of Ireland as opposed to the far more common
trooping faeries. Most tales speak of encounters with
single leprechauns so it is clear they enjoy their own
company, but they also have their sociable moments
– their family life, clan loyalties and so on – which
are what we are more interested in. Leprechauns
are less domesticated when it comes to adopting
human households than, say, the brownies of
Scotland or the kobolds of Germany, or their
relations in many other countries, but they have been
known to attach themselves to human families and
even follow them when they move, which is how
there come to be leprechauns in places like North
America and Australia.

Most leprechauns live in Ireland though, where they
have evolved a quite distinct identity from the Little
People of neighbouring countries. In general they are
more independent of humans, more interested in gold
and more witty than other Little People. Until a
century or two ago no-one in Ireland doubted them
any more than they doubted the existence of the Pope
in Rome. In the first years of the twentieth century a
famous scholar named Evans Wentz was impressed by
the stir in Mullingar over a leprechaun who had
apparently been parading himself before half the
children of the parish, and many of the grown people
too. Everyone was out looking to catch it. Then the
rumour spread that it had been caught by the local
police. But when the scholar, continuing on his
travels, told this rumour to an old man at Ballywillan
where he stopped for the night, the old man laughed
and said: 'Now that couldn't be at all, for everybody

The owl, as is well known, is an almost supernatural creature itself. Certainly it is the closest of all birds to the faery world and is used by leprechauns to get from here to there at times. But the owl is a proud creature with affairs of its own to attend to and the leprechaun usually has to resort to less comfortable means of transport – such as dogs, sheep or horses; or even Shanks' Pony.

A farmer can tell when a leprechaun has been riding one of his beasts all night by the mud on him in the morning, and his exhaustion. This is particularly common in Clare and Galway where leprechauns are fond of organized races with horses, sheep, goats and even dogs. So if you see such animals racing round in circles at night you'll now know what is going on.

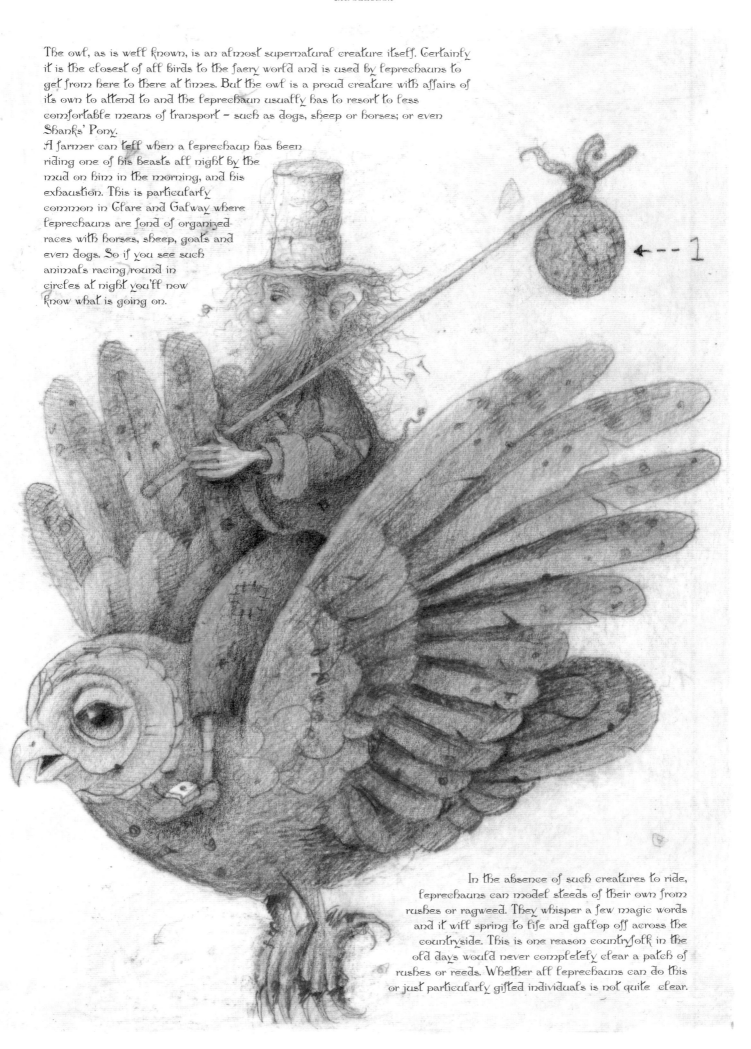

← - - - 1

In the absence of such creatures to ride, leprechauns can model steeds of their own from rushes or ragweed. They whisper a few magic words and it will spring to life and gallop off across the countryside. This is one reason countryfolk in the old days would never completely clear a patch of rushes or reeds. Whether all leprechauns can do this or just particularly gifted individuals is not quite clear.

'They have many other talents besides.'

1. Fiddler's bow
2. Ladle
3. Pot
4. Jack-in-the-Box, for the origins
of which see Kobolds (p. 92)

knows the leprechaun is a spirit and can't be caught by any blessed policeman, though it is likely one might get his gold if they got him cornered so that he had no chance to run away.'

In those days even judges could still confess openly to having met leprechauns without much fear of being laughed off the Bench. There is more scepticism now. In fact, to be perfectly truthful, most people in Ireland today do not seriously believe in leprechauns at all, however partial they may be to the idea of them. And there are those who find the whole subject embarrassing because it reminds them of aspects of the past they would rather forget. Which is fair enough really. Each to his own. Leprechauns themselves are quite happy with this state of affairs. It means there is that much less chance of being rudely interrupted while working away under the hedgerow by some great human eager to squeeze your treasure out of you. And it is easier to play tricks when your victim is unaware of your existence.

Because they are a kind of faery, leprechauns are often invisible. They may pass by as a swirl of dust, so in the old days men would raise their hats and women curtsey if a pillar of dust blew by, just in case. If you throw your left shoe at the cloud and it is really a leprechaun, he has to drop whatever he is holding, including any bags of gold; but if he is not holding anything, you may just gain his ill-will from it.

In the old days people would also leave out a dish of milk or fresh water at night for leprechauns, avoid cutting down hawthorn or whitethorn bushes, leave the dregs in their glasses when going to bed, and many other little courtesies to keep in with them. That so few people now take the trouble is the cause of endless bad luck which might otherwise be happily avoided.

Leprechauns have been known to 'adopt' families and move in with them, though this is rarer than with the Little People of other countries. Often the first sign that a leprechaun has moved in is that things start to go missing, or turn up in unexpected places. Sometimes even a table or a chair might be thrown across the room, and the whiskey or milk will be found to have gone down overnight, or to have been topped up with water. If all this happens, the family will know they must start leaving out little presents of food and drink and anything else that might take the little fellow's fancy. Then, with luck, instead of doing mischief the leprechaun will go round the house and barns at night finishing off jobs that the big people have had no time to do.

All this can happen without the family clapping eyes on their guest. But those who have seen or met a leprechaun most often describe him (it nearly always is a 'him') as being two to three feet tall, with a wizened face, bright eyes and a red nose. His dress varies but tends to be old-fashioned, in mainly greens and browns with touches of bright red, and often shabby. Some people have met leprechauns only a few inches tall while others seemed barely shorter than humans, but usually their size falls somewhere in between. This is because their form is more flexible than ours. They can even adopt the shape of animals, it is said, which you can tell by the strange behaviour of the creature, especially if it talks to you.

One sure way of seeing leprechauns is to carry a sprig of four-leaf clover or shamrock somewhere about your person, or a stone with a natural hole bored through it, or a piece of wood with a knot that has been knocked out. Some say a sprig of the faery cap flower (also known as lusmore or foxglove) conveys the same power, but this is disputed. Often also the robin redbreast will lead you to a leprechaun because they are great friends. In fact a robin is the most common bird form the leprechaun will adopt, for which reason it is especially bad luck to kill or trap a robin, even accidentally.

THERE IS A SENTIMENTAL notion abroad of leprechauns being bright, sunny little folk only too eager to surrender their pots of gold to passing strangers, but this is far from the truth. It has been known to happen, but it is rare. Leprechauns are great misers, and like all misers they do not just collect gold for the sake of giving it away to passing strangers, not without good cause anyway. As to being cheerful, well some leprechauns are and some aren't, purely as a matter of temperament. But however sunny their disposition, it may well not be apparent to one of us. Since most humans have only ever really been interested in leprechauns for the sake of their gold, we should not be too surprised if they are wary of us and perhaps harbouring a few grievances.

So the thing to remember about leprechauns should you happen to meet one is that they can be as nice as pie, but they may also seem cantankerous, vindictive, spiteful old curmudgeons, or anything in between. A bit like humans really. But on the whole they tend more towards mischief. They love pranks, especially if there is a lesson in it for the victim. So when meeting a leprechaun it is best to be courteous and friendly. And think twice before accepting any gift that is freely offered.

The first leprechauns are said to have been the offspring of faeries and bogeymen. This means they have a bit of both in them, and you cannot be sure how much till you get to know your leprechaun. However, it is fair to say that real evil in a leprechaun is as rare as pure kindness. If some of their pranks seem wholly malicious, it is generally because they have different values to us. In Scotland, however, the Brownie (a close cousin of the leprechaun) is liable to turn into a boggart when offended, and a boggart can be really wicked.

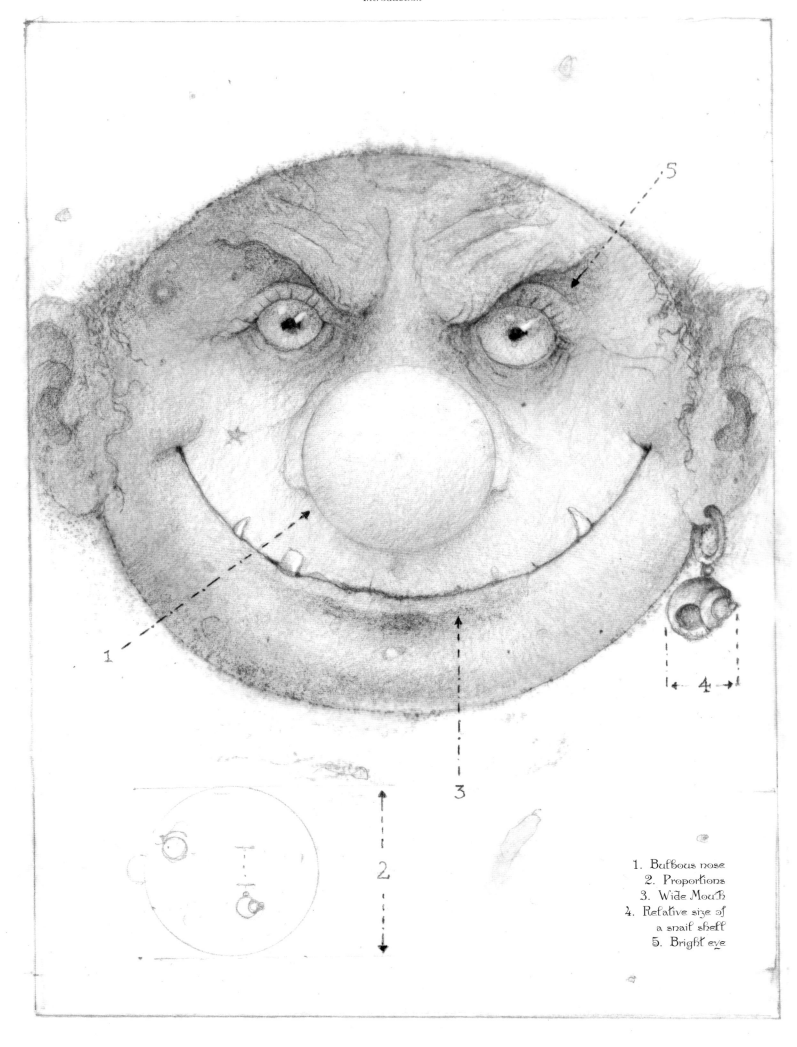

1. Bulbous nose
2. Proportions
3. Wide Mouth
4. Relative size of
   a snail shell
5. Bright eye

Chapter One
habits & habitat

THERE ARE MANY SUGGESTIONS FOR the origin of the word leprechaun. Lady Gregory and W. B. Yeats believed it came from *leith broghan*, 'the shoe maker', or even 'the one-shoe maker', because the leprechaun is usually seen working on just the one shoe, or brogue. Others say it comes from *luchorpan* or small-bodied fellow. Still others suggest it comes from *luacharman*, the Irish for 'pygmy'; or possibly, since *luachair* means 'rush', it means 'rushyman'.

You can take your pick which to believe, or perhaps they are all true at the same time, which would be in keeping with the nature of leprechauns. And then, of course, the term 'leprechaun' strictly applies only to the Little People of Leinster province around Dublin. Elsewhere they have other names. In Munster province they are known as luricaunes or cluricaunes, in Tipperary lurigadaunes and in Kildare luriceen. In Ulster province they are called logherymen or luchrymen.

For simplicity we mostly call them all leprechauns in this book, because it would be too confusing otherwise. And although they see themselves as very different, the truth is that to the outsider the differences between the clans are not glaringly obvious; except perhaps with the cluricaunes of Munster who have a reputation for wildness. So we will mostly call them all leprechauns, but just remember not to call one a leprechaun to its face unless you happen to be in Leinster.

As to personal names, leprechauns are very secretive about these. As in the German story of Rumpelstiltskin, to know the true name of one of the faery folk is to gain power over them; or at least to become immune to any power they have over you. Most names that have become known to us are nicknames or 'use' names which they have often borrowed from humans, but leprechauns are cagey even about these.

Telltale Signs

 E HAVE MENTIONED SIGNS that show if a leprechaun has moved into your home, but they are most often met with out in the country, near clear springs or among tall rushes or under a hedgerow, particularly in the early evening. The thing to listen out for is the tapping of the leprechaun's little hammer as he works away on a shoe. This is your most likely signal because they blend so well into the background. Even though they are not actually invisible, you could easily pass right by one without noticing. Often though, they have a bit of bright red in their clothing, which may catch your eye and give them away.

Anyway, once you think there is a leprechaun nearby, you must creep up on him quieter than a mouse if he is not to hear you coming and vanish. Leprechauns have wonderfully sharp hearing and move silently themselves, but luckily they also get engrossed in what they are doing and this makes them careless. It helps if they are singing or whistling as they work, which they often do, as this will both guide you to them and cover the noise of your approach.

Dwellings

 ON THE WHOLE LEPRECHAUNS prefer to adapt somewhere to their needs rather than build a house from scratch. If they have not attached themselves to some human habitation, an abandoned burrow or beehive, hollow tree or snug cave is their usual choice. Not only does this save time for more profitable and interesting occupations, but it takes very little 'glamour' to blend their homes so completely into the landscape that you can be standing a few feet away and not see what it is you are looking at. They often make their homes in the depth of thorn bushes, which is why such bushes are best not disturbed.

Because of their fondness for buried treasure, leprechauns like to make their homes near ancient burial mounds and are often met in such neighbourhoods. But there are far more leprechauns than 'faery mounds', and other faeries are also attracted to them, so for the sake of a quiet life they are scattered far and wide across the countryside.

Mushrooms are famously associated with faeries of all kinds, and leprechauns are no exception. Faery rings are among their favourite meeting places and it is said that if you put one foot in the ring while leprechauns are invisibly gathered there, you will be able to see them clearly. But if you put both feet in you may become their prisoner and have to obey their every command. Unless you have somehow offended them there is no great danger in this, they will only have a laugh at your expense. But you may well come to your senses later feeling a mite battered and bruised, and with no idea at all of how you got that way, or where the day or night has gone.

Only the smallest leprechauns actually make their homes in mushrooms and toadstools, as we see here, and then only in the

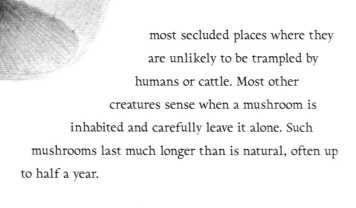

most secluded places where they are unlikely to be trampled by humans or cattle. Most other creatures sense when a mushroom is inhabited and carefully leave it alone. Such mushrooms last much longer than is natural, often up to half a year.

From Scotland, where they have very similar traditions about the faeries and Little People to those prevailing in Ireland (though the Scots always seem to have been much more wary of them), comes a sweet tale that shows how seriously people once took those beliefs.

In 1831 a labourer was walking along the shore near Uig on the Isle of Lewis when he noticed that rough weather had washed away a sandbank, exposing a cave. Natural curiosity led him to poke his head in, and what should he see but a curious beehive-shaped object like a little house made of clay.

Thinking there might be treasure in it, he smashed the thing with his spade and to his horror saw dozens of tiny people inside. Terrified of the rage of the Little People, he ran off; but his wife was made of sterner stuff and forced him to go back. What they found was that the Little People, ninety-three of them, were in fact carved from walrus ivory and these have since become famous as the Lewis Chessmen, dating from the eleventh or twelfth century AD. Many are now on show in the British Museum and are widely on sale as reproductions. It is surmised that they were the hoard of a travelling ivory salesman who perhaps hid them in the cave and never had the chance to retrieve them.

Fashions

As with any other people, the dressing habits and fashions of leprechauns vary from province to province in Ireland, but there are generalizations we can make without too much fear of contradiction.

Leprechauns fiercely deny being influenced in their dress by human fashions but they obviously are, only it takes a hundred years or so to show. And often another hundred before the more conservative elements start to bend. So shoes with enormous silver buckles and three-cornered hats are still quite the thing among leprechauns, and stovepipe hats have yet to peak in popularity. But you are unlikely to see a leprechaun wearing trainers and a reversed baseball cap (except at Halloween when they like to dress up as humans to frighten each other). Red 'nightcaps' are probably still the most common form of headgear, but it can be almost anything. Red is a popular colour anyway as a contrast to the more common greens and browns, the red dye being extracted from lichen. Blue is spoken of sometimes, but among leprechauns it is considered a rather bold fashion statement bordering on eccentricity. Despite the variety in their dress, it is easy enough to recognize a leprechaun when you meet one. They are obviously not, for example, nymphs or dryads. Some might be mistaken for dwarfs or bogeymen, but dwarfs are strangely absent from Ireland and bogeymen have no sense of humour.

Shoes are the leprechaun's craft speciality. In ancient times their own shoes and boots were made from metal for the sake of durability, which is how they became tinkers as well as shoemakers; but they have gradually been weaned to more comfortable habits. These days their shoes are generally leather, and for the other faeries they make the most exquisite little slippers of embroidered silk.

Whatever the material, high heels are popular with leprechauns because although they claim to be quite happy with their stature, they are more sensitive about it than they let on. They have magical ways of making themselves taller, of course, but, as with shape-shifting and going invisible, it takes effort to maintain for any length of time.

Dressing up at Halloween is even more popular with leprechauns than humans. Being shape-shifters, they have the advantage too in being able to exaggerate their looks without much need of masks or make-up.

Metal hats are not common with leprechauns but anything goes, really, when it comes to headwear. Here we see a leprechaun candlestick maker showing off his wares. His hat is a dual-purpose helmet and candle-holder for underground exploration.

Food

LEPRECHAUNS' TASTE IN FOOD IS VERY similar to ours but there are certain items peculiar to them. The roots of the silver weed (*brisgein*) are considered a particular delicacy, although humans gave up eating it when potatoes came along. Heather tops are a popular herb for cooking and are also brewed into a kind of ale. Heather stems and roots are sometimes chewed by leprechauns much as we would chew liquorice. Mushrooms and toadstools (many of which are poisonous to us) are also naturally among their favourite comestibles, plus 'fairy butter', a fungus that grows round the base of trees.

Leprechauns are quite solitary by inclination. They also have old-fashioned notions about the division of labour. Put these two together and what you get is a lot of hungry and homeless leprechaun bachelors. This is why so many people imagine all leprechauns are male. It is also what sometimes compels them to adopt human households and live off the scraps left out for them.

Female leprechauns are wonderful cooks and use many more herbs in their dishes than we do. Occasionally when wandering the Irish countryside you will catch delicious scents of their baking when no house can be seen for miles. You can tell it's leprechaun cooking because although you will not quite know what it is you are smelling, you will become suddenly ravenous, but however hard you look you cannot find where it is coming from.

Drink

When lords and ladies were common in Ireland, it was also common for leprechauns to take up residence in their cellars and help themselves from the stock. Leprechauns hate tight-fistedness in others so if one was begrudged his share (as he saw it), he could turn nasty and make his hosts' lives a misery. Even worse, if the leprechaun was driven away by his host's rudeness he might turn all the contents of the cellar to sea water. The wise lord welcomed his leprechaun and in return for the hospitality, the leprechaun would place charms on the barrels and bottles to keep the contents sweet, and bring luck to the household generally.

More humble folk also acquire leprechaun lodgers so, just in case, the etiquette is never to complain if you spill a drink, but say: 'And that's a drop for you, my good fellow.' Because it may have been he that jogged your hand on account of being thirsty.

Leprechauns enjoy much the same drinks as we do. Spring water is their favourite thirst quencher, followed by tea and milk. They are especially fond of goat's and deer's milk, the latter given in return for warning of hunters. Most leprechauns are also partial to whiskey, wine, mead and beer. The cluricaunes of Munster are said to be over-partial to them, but this is probably an uncharitable slur put about by their neighbours.

CLURICAUNE.

Opposite: The secret of making whiskey or usquebaugh, 'Water of Life', was given to the world by the Tuatha. Leprechauns are great brewers and distillers, and can turn out as fine a drop of whiskey as anyone. But they generally prefer to make poteen or Uisce Poitín, 'little pot whiskey', which is brewed in smaller quantities and to more imaginative recipes. The basic ingredients are grains like barley, and often potatoes, but beyond that anything goes; each leprechaun is on his own and in fierce competition with every other leprechaun to produce the most interesting. Winning recipes are as jealously guarded as gold.

UISCE POITIN.

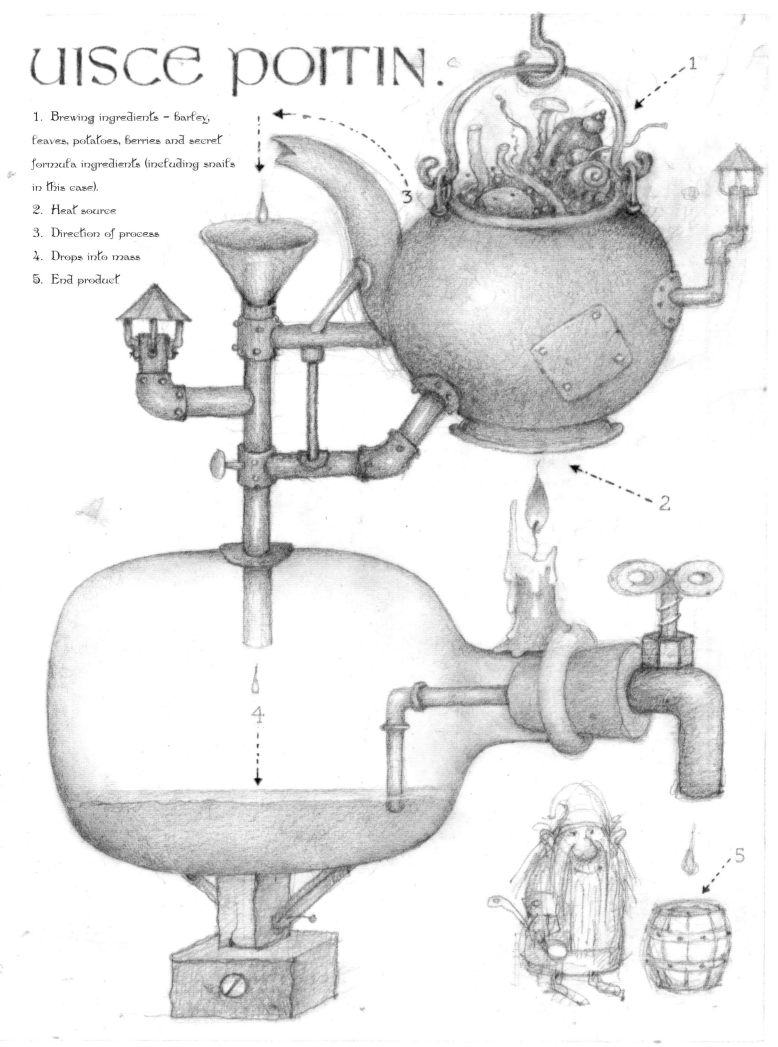

1. Brewing ingredients – barley, leaves, potatoes, berries and secret formula ingredients (including snails in this case).
2. Heat source
3. Direction of process
4. Drops into mass
5. End product

Work

GOLD IS THE GREAT LOVE OF leprechauns and when not shoemaking, tinkering or tailoring to earn it from the other faeries, they go hunting for buried treasure. They do not always dig it up though; once they find the location of buried treasure they are often happy just to know where it is. After all, they would only have to bury it again elsewhere. So they unearth it only if there seems a danger of it being found by others, or if it needs to be shared out among the finders.

Unlike with most of us, gold is not seen as a means to an end (i.e. buying lots of luxuries). Leprechauns enjoy treasure simply for its own sake. They have no great wish to convert it into other things because they are generally quite content with their modest lot (apart from their store of gold, that is). Some philosophers have speculated that gold is somehow the cause of leprechauns' extreme longevity and that this is why they prize it so much. But leprechauns themselves have little to say on the subject, least of all to humans.

As with all faery creatures, leprechauns are especially lively on nights of the full moon, and below we see a party of them heading home from a successful treasure hunt. Leprechauns often go treasure hunting in bands. This goes slightly against the grain of their nature, but it so happens that several leprechauns together are far more sensitive to the presence of gold than they are individually, so this brings them together.

Five is considered the ideal number for treasure hunting. To limit arguments, one leprechaun is elected leader for the night and called 'Himself'. He occasionally dons a makeshift crown to denote his authority, but has to be careful not to push his luck too far because all leprechauns hate being ordered about much. Himself gets to carry the treasure home if it is found, and the blame if it is not. In this case they have been so lucky that two of them are carrying the treasure between them, but this is exceptional.

Work

IT IS OF COURSE LEPRECHAUNS WHO GO OFF WITH THE JEWELLERY and other precious things people drop by the wayside in Ireland. But if, say, a ring is of particular sentimental value, they can usually be prevailed upon to return it if the owner leaves something of greater worth near where it was lost. You might imagine the leprechauns would simply pocket this too but, for all their mischief, leprechauns have a great sense of honour. They may believe in 'finders keepers, losers weepers' and it is a common prejudice among them that people only lose things they are no longer very attached to, but most leprechauns are not hard-hearted. They recognize sincerity when they meet it, and within their own terms are perfectly honest. There are a few rogues, of course, but they are rare and unpopular among their own kind.

Opposite we see a female leprechaun with her collection of 'found' jewellery gathered over the centuries. The necklace originally belonged to a countess out riding on a moonlight tryst with a secret lover. As she could not admit to where and how she had lost it, the countess blamed its disappearance on the leprechaun living in their cellar, which to those who found the necklace seemed justification enough for holding on to it.

Female leprechauns are as deft with their fingers as the males, and they make dresses for the other faeries as well as themselves. On the whole they take more care with their appearance than the males and can dress quite prettily. Their favourite colour is green, but they like to offset it with other colours, particularly red and mauve.

For buttons, brooches and other decorations, female leprechauns collect dead insects which they soak in a kind of quick-drying amber that hardens to almost the strength of steel.

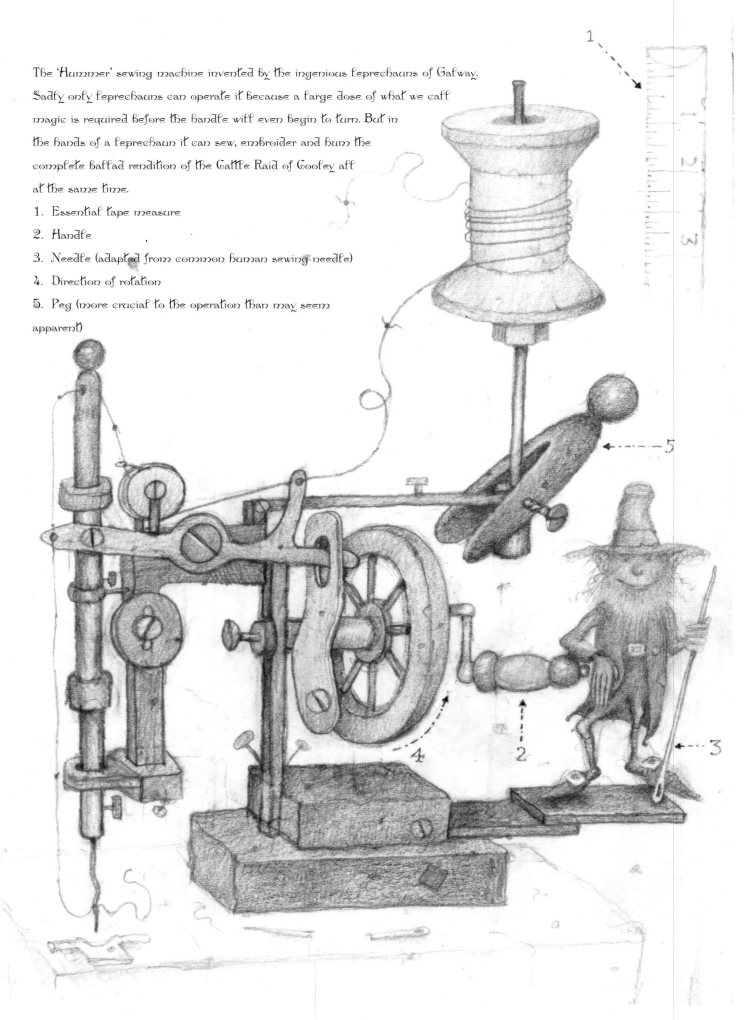

The 'Hummer' sewing machine invented by the ingenious leprechauns of Galway.
Sadly only leprechauns can operate it because a large dose of what we call
magic is required before the handle will even begin to turn. But in
the hands of a leprechaun it can sew, embroider and hum the
complete ballad rendition of the Cattle Raid of Cooley all
at the same time.

1. Essential tape measure

2. Handle

3. Needle (adapted from common human sewing needle)

4. Direction of rotation

5. Peg (more crucial to the operation than may seem
apparent)

IME IS A MECHANISM WHOSE inner workings hold few mysteries for the leprechaun, so watches and clocks pose even fewer problems. The secret of many a successful clockmaker in the old days was to have a friendly leprechaun to deal with all the problematic cases, the sick old clocks that would just not keep going.

Size is a great help, of course, when it comes to sorting all those tiny cogs and wheels, but leprechauns also have a great natural affinity with clockwork, as opposed to electronics, which most have still to come to terms with. This is not all that surprising since most have still not forgiven the electric light bulb for driving the shadows (and consequently them) out of human homes; but the chances are that once leprechauns begin to take an interest, no electronic machine will be safe from them. In fact there are rumours that with computers it is happening already.

Leprechauns have been known to carry watches which they appear to consult for the time, but this is just a kind of ongoing joke. What they are in fact checking is how slow or fast the watch is compared with what they just innately know to be the time.

'Borrowing' is considered a perfectly respectable activity among leprechauns, and quite distinct from stealing, since the intention is always to return whatever is taken at some point, or pay the owner back some other way.

This is a tricky area of ethics that really is best not enquired into too deeply. Often leprechauns 'borrow' things just to annoy humans who irritate them, and often they forget to return things they have borrowed. So from our point of view the distinction can seem a bit arbitrary. But there is no point getting annoyed about it. If things start to go missing, your best bet is simply to make an effort to get on the right side of your leprechaun. Start leaving out little gifts for him and dropping compliments when he might be in earshot, along with hints about whatever has gone missing. Leprechauns may be mischievous and wary of us, but they actually quite enjoy getting along with human beings.

Jewellery making is a natural extension of the leprechauns' other talents, so much of their jewellery is original rather than 'borrowed' from humans. And some jewellery that people wear is of course of leprechaun origin, though this is now much less common than in the days when antique jewellery was often worn by the rich. That's one of the things about leprechaun jewellery, it usually looks antique even when brand new.

Leprechauns have a particular fondness for pearls, partly because of the poetic way they are formed, and partly for their resemblance to the moon. So there is a great trade between leprechauns and sea-sprites, whose special fondness is for mead.

Courtship

TYING A KNOT IN A ROSE stem or bramble is taken as a great compliment by leprechaun ladies, and if you have tried doing this yourself you will appreciate why. Some leprechaun males take the easy way by talking the rose into tying itself up, convincing the poor flower that the sun is going round in complicated circles; but this is quite rightly considered cheating and the females have ways of determining if it has happened.

The ultimate rejection of a would-be suitor is the female to cut through the knot and return the gift.

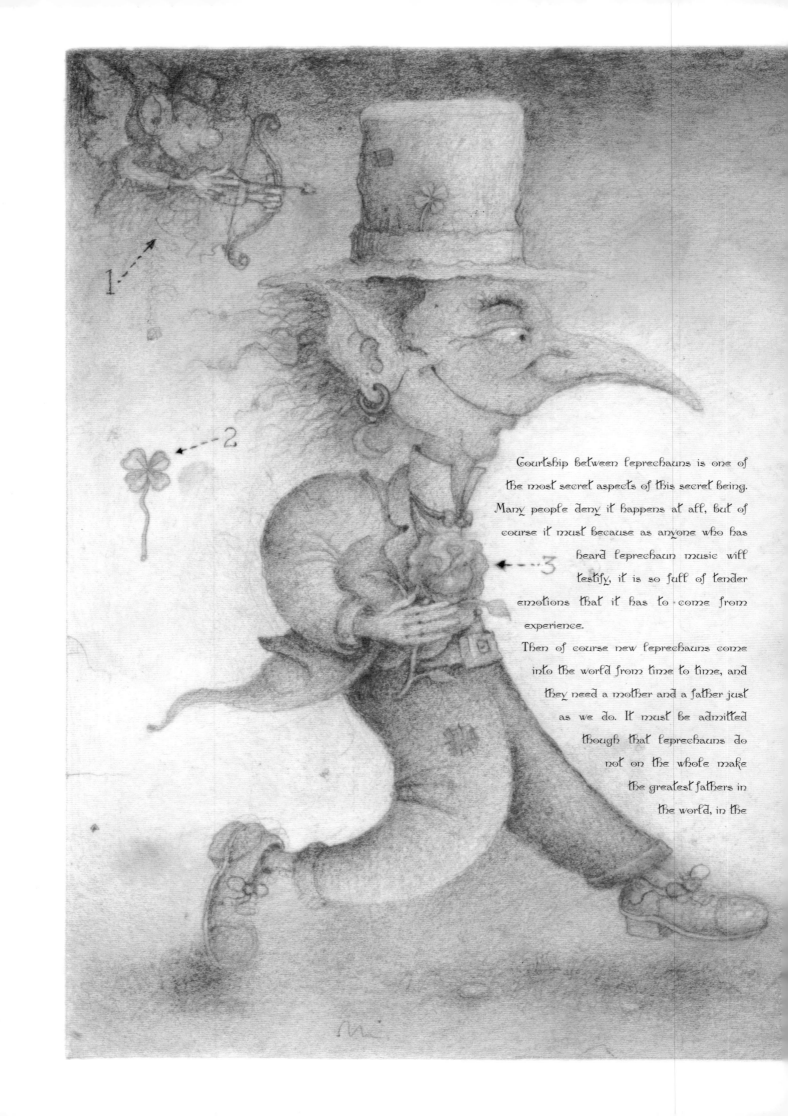

Courtship between leprechauns is one of the most secret aspects of this secret being. Many people deny it happens at all, but of course it must because as anyone who has heard leprechaun music will testify, it is so full of tender emotions that it has to come from experience.

Then of course new leprechauns come into the world from time to time, and they need a mother and a father just as we do. It must be admitted though that leprechauns do not on the whole make the greatest fathers in the world, in the

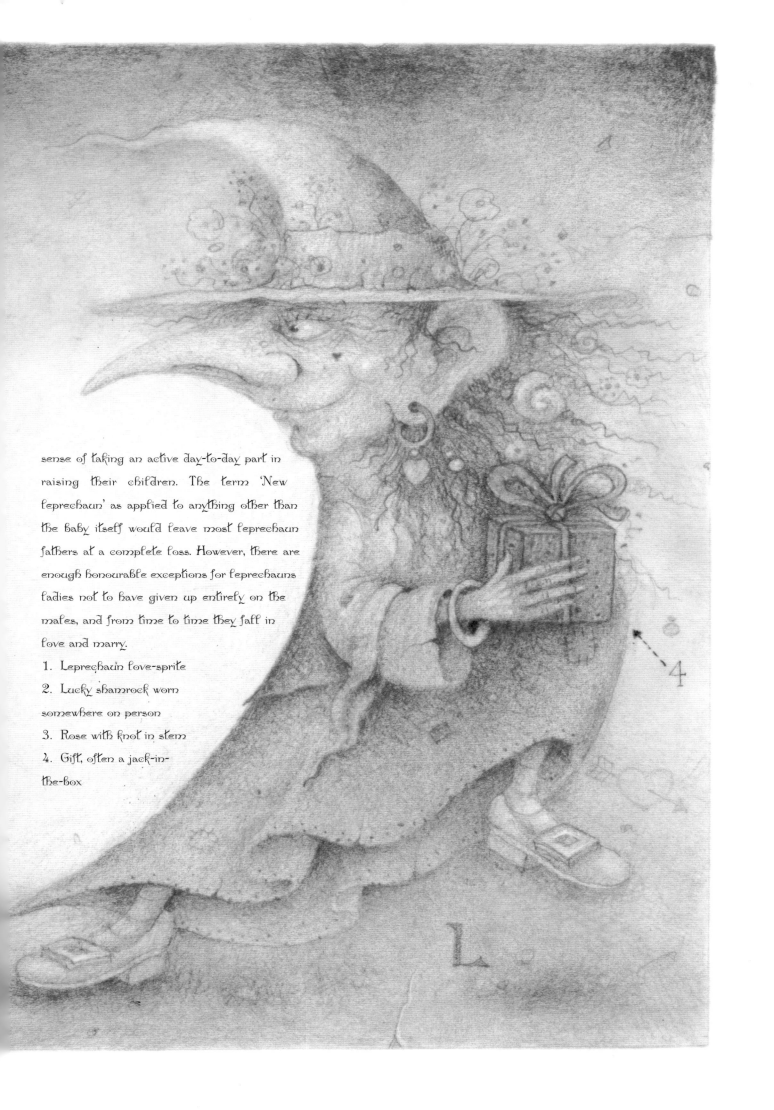

sense of taking an active day-to-day part in raising their children. The term 'New leprechaun' as applied to anything other than the baby itself would leave most leprechaun fathers at a complete loss. However, there are enough honourable exceptions for leprechauns ladies not to have given up entirely on the males, and from time to time they fall in love and marry.

1. Leprechaun love-sprite
2. Lucky shamrock worn somewhere on person
3. Rose with knot in stem
4. Gift, often a jack-in-the-box

Catching Leprechauns

I T IS WELL KNOWN THAT DESPITE their generally poverty-stricken demeanour most leprechauns are as rich as Croesus. In fact, as some philosopher said, a leprechaun without a pot of gold is like a rose without perfume – as sad but also as unlikely. If they don't have a pot of gold they will have a magic purse that can never be emptied, or else they know the whereabouts of buried treasure. They can be forced to surrender one of these prizes if only you catch one of the little fellows and hold him fast. There are one or two stories of generous leprechauns who have delivered up their gold from the pure kindness of their hearts, but the common wisdom in Ireland is that if you want a leprechaun's treasure, you have to extract it from him by force.

The trickiest bit has always been catching the leprechaun in the first place. Your best bet, if you come upon one under a bush at sunset, tapping away at his last and whistling while he works, is simply to creep up as quick as a squirrel and catch him before he realizes what you are about. Then if you hold him tight and don't take your eyes off him, he will have to give what you demand. But with the cunning of their words, leprechauns are as slippery as eels to keep hold of; and if you take your eyes off them for a second, even to blink, they are likely to vanish.

Even if you succeed in all this, in finding the leprechaun, catching him and extracting from him some pledge of a prize, you are still likely to come unstuck somehow. For instance there is the tale of Tim O'Donovan of Kerry who succeeded in forcing a leprechaun to show him a spot in a bog where treasure was buried. Only of course Tim had no spade with him, so he marked the spot by driving a stick into the ground and leaving his hat perched on it. But the next morning when he came back what should he find but a hundred sticks all over the bog, each with a hat on it so much like his own that he could not tell them apart and had to go home again empty handed.

Something to remember if you succeed in persuading a leprechaun to show or tell you where treasure is buried, is not to reveal the secret to a living soul before you have it safely dug up and deposited in a bank, or else it will vanish. Some say that even then it is likely to turn to dust if you reveal how you came by it, but others contradict this. To be on the safe side it is perhaps best to claim that a metal detector pointed the way.

Not many people have ever got the better of a leprechaun, though in theory it should be possible. They are bound by honesty and if they give a pledge they must stick to it. The trickiness comes in the wording of the pledge. Likewise, the leprechaun in the last story could not just remove the stick and hat when Tim O'Donovan went away for his spade. That would be breaking their compact, so another way had to be found.

Because they are so true to their own code of honour (strange though that code may often seem to us) leprechauns get furious when humans fail to honour their own side of a bargain. And they make uncomfortable enemies.

Instead of treasure, leprechauns will sometimes offer three wishes when captured. Being masters of what we call magic, they are quite able to deliver almost any request. Trick wishes, such as immediately asking for ten more, will only be met with scorn, but almost anything else goes. The wisest gifts to ask for are intangible blessings like talent, luck and good health, because these do not force the mould of nature. But few people are able to think this clearly in the heat of the moment, and their more superficial wishes have a strange habit of backfiring.

So be careful if you ever get to play this game with a leprechaun, because they are responsible for the old saying 'Be careful with your wishes, because they may come true'. Beware also of accepting a fourth wish if you succeed in obtaining the three, because it is certain to undo all that went before.

Bottling Leprechauns

LTHOUGH IT IS NOT COMMON, THERE IS A BELIEF IN circulation that the surest way of capturing a leprechaun is to bottle him, because once you have him trapped in a bottle you no longer need to keep tight hold, or your eye fixed on him. Then you can take your time in framing your wishes or extracting promises or gold and are less likely to be tricked. The problem, of course, is getting him into the bottle.

A gold coin is generally the best bait for the trap, but lacking that a measure of whiskey may do the trick. Or if it has been noticed that a certain food has been going missing from the pantry, a piece of this will do. Then the thing to do is leave the jar or bottle somewhere innocent seeming, but with a hiding place nearby for you to watch and wait.

It all sounds very beguiling but we have yet to find a solid instance of anyone claiming to have actually caught a leprechaun this way.

Chapter Two
Customs and Culture

HE TWO GREATEST FESTIVALS IN the leprechauns' calendar are May Eve and Halloween, which divide the year for them into its warm and cool halves and are times when leprechauns often move house to make the best of the weather. On the eve of 1 May they congregate at special places all over the country for great celebrations with singing and dancing and no end of other entertainments. The greatest feast of all is the Beltane Fair of Uisnech in County Westmeath. This is where leprechauns from opposite ends of Ireland most often meet to exchange songs and riddles and stories. It is a great melting pot of all the leprechauns of Ireland, and a great place for

settling disputes between them. At the Beltane Fair is also held a great marriage ball where single leprechauns gather to court others from distant parts, if that is their inclination.

May Eve marks the start of summer and is a time of optimism, rejoicing and looking forward to new things. Halloween marks the start of winter and although it is a celebration of the year's harvest and all that kind of thing, the mood is more sombre and reflective. Halloween is also a time of mischief because, as everyone knows, on that night the gates between the otherworld and this one are thrown wide open and all kinds of unsettling creatures walk abroad.

Opposite: Leprechauns are not great ones for kings and queens, but on occasions such as the Beltane Fair of Uisnech they may elect a couple to preside over the celebrations and decide any disputes brought before them. Any judgement they make is binding for a year, but that is about as seriously as the business is taken. When the fair is over, the king and queen go back to normal leprechaun life and someone else will be elected next time.

Leprechauns themselves are not really that greatly bothered by the likes of the banshee, the morrigan and the rest, because they know well enough how to keep out of their way. They know the places to avoid on Halloween and how to escape any serious bogle they should happen to run into. Mostly anyway. And besides all this, it is a night when they are licensed to behave as wildly as they like themselves, so in a sense they are part of the mayhem.

Besides playing pranks on humans and each other at Halloween, leprechauns gather for parties, though in smaller numbers than on May Eve and in more scattered places. Halloween is a particularly good night for fortune telling, though not for treasure hunting because of all the other creatures that get attracted by treasure hoards. Hazelnuts and apples are the particular delicacies of Halloween.

May Eve and Halloween are the two greatest leprechaun festivals, but they have many others. About every six weeks in fact there is a major cause for festival. After Halloween comes Yuletide, then St Brigid's Day (1 February, also called Candlemas), St Patrick's Day (17 March), May Eve, Midsummer Day, Harvest Festival (1 August), Evens Eve (21 September) and then back to Halloween.

It may seem a bit strange that leprechauns celebrate saints' days when they are not strictly speaking Christians at all, but there are two reasons for this. One is that they fall on days when it is natural for leprechauns to celebrate anyway (such as St Brigid's Day, which for them marks the end of winter and the beginning of spring). And then there is the mostly cordial relationship that has always existed in Ireland between the Church and the faeries, relatively speaking. It has not always been completely cordial, of course, there have been ups and downs, but compared with most other places the Church in Ireland has always respected the faeries, and they have returned the favour.

St Patrick's Day falls close enough to the spring equinox anyway for leprechauns to have adopted it as a festival of their own. And like most of the Irish they have a special affection for the good Patrick, along with Brigid and Columcille.

Festivals are where all the latest gossip is shared and news broadcast by criers such as this one.

1. Handbell for attracting attention

2. Quill for inscribing the scroll. Because leprechaun scribes get so carried away with initial letters, this is often as far as a scroll gets. The rest has to be delivered from memory.

3. That is the case here, and because he is so proud of his handiwork, the crier is going around with the scroll held upside down for his audience to admire his initial letter.

Games

Festivals are the main social events in the leprechauns' otherwise solitary lives. They are also the occasion for sporting events and many other games and entertainments.

'Clanger' McGuire from Tyrone, three times All Ireland Fleaweight Champion; unbeaten holder of the Shamrock Belt for the most knockouts in the Beltane Tournament of Uisnech (five in as many fights. The remaining contenders all suddenly remembered they had pressing family matters to attend to – principally ensuring their personal survival for the sake of their nearest and dearest – and took to the hills). 'Clanger' gained his nickname from the resounding ring of his knockout punches. He was forced to retire under a cloud when it was discovered where he was in the habit of keeping his most lucky horseshoe.

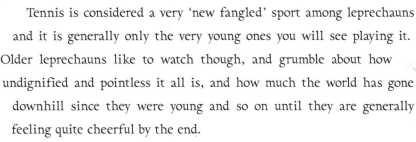

Tennis is considered a very 'new fangled' sport among leprechauns and it is generally only the very young ones you will see playing it. Older leprechauns like to watch though, and grumble about how undignified and pointless it all is, and how much the world has gone downhill since they were young and so on until they are generally feeling quite cheerful by the end.

A particular problem for umpires at leprechaun tennis matches is determining when the players are using magic to make the ball go (or come) where they want. Neutrality is also something easily called into question. In this case, as is common, a piskie from Cornwall across the water has been called in to arbitrate.

Hurling dates back to before recorded history. There have been periodic attempts to ban it since the time of the Normans because of the riots and even wars it has started, but the game has survived to become the second most popular sport in Ireland today, played regularly by over one tenth of a quarter of the population, which is quite a sizeable fraction when you stop to think about it. These days the rules, for humans anyway, are quite tame compared to what they were. Not that there were many rules, that is the point. At one time the only rule was that whichever team got the ball to a certain spot was the winner. Otherwise anything went, and anyone who felt up to it could join in. Sometimes the players forgot even this one rule in the excitement of settling old scores and hurling matches often degenerated rapidly into full-scale battle between one community and the next.

Leprechauns like to play the game in the old-fashioned way with no nonsense about 'correct' tackling and so on. One of their few concessions to modern developments in the human game is to adopt an almost standard stick instead of just taking along whatever weapon they most fancied, as this led to too many disputes before the game even began.

A little island at the Ballyhefaan ford near Kilworth in County Cork was once famous for leprechaun hurling matches played there under the full moon, one team wearing red scarves tied round their heads, the other with white.

Magpie

IN ANCIENT IRELAND THERE WERE TWO famous board games mentioned in the legends – Fidchell and Brandubh. Fidchell (Wooden Wisdom) was invented by the Tuatha de Danaan and among mortals only royalty and druids were permitted to play. Brandubh, or Black Raven, was open to anyone, noble and peasant alike. Mostly these games were played for the same reasons people play chess and draughts today, or any other such game for that matter. But they also had a more serious side, a mystical dimension. Sometimes the fate of nations hung on the outcome of a game, or the future could be read in its progress. So they believed anyway, and who can say for sure that this was not once so?

The game Brandubh is closely related to the Tafl games of Scandinavia but was played in Ireland long before the Vikings came, so its origins are obscure. As the name Black Raven suggests, it is a war game. At the start a king and his four champions are surrounded by eight enemies, and either the king escapes the board or he is caught and the enemy wins. The board is seven spaces square. Larger boards with more playing pieces were used elsewhere, and even occasionally in Ireland, but the 7 x 7 board was the most popular, and the neatest in symbolism. The king piece represents the High King of Ireland surrounded by the four kings or fighting queens of Munster, Leinster, Ulster and Connaught. All very neatly symbolic.

Among mortals in Ireland Brandubh was a favourite game for a thousand or so years, maybe longer, but then it fell from favour and has since become almost forgotten. Leprechauns, however, having longer memories and slower-moving tastes than us, continue to play it with enthusiasm to this day, though with a few changes to suit it better to themselves.

To begin with they don't think of the game much in terms of kings and queens and battles for sovereignty, since leprechauns have little interest in such things. They see the king as a leprechaun they call 'Himself' carrying a pot of gold and surrounded by four friends, a treasure-hunting party heading home after a successful night. They in turn are surrounded by eight rivals who want to grab the gold for themselves. (If you're playing the rivals' part you see it as trying to recapture your own stolen treasure which the others happen to have stumbled upon.) Otherwise the game is much the same, though a couple of minor rules seem unique to leprechauns. Perhaps these are what make the 'king' piece, or Himself, move much as you would expect of a leprechaun carrying a pot of gold – slowly but defending it like a bear with cubs.

Leprechauns have also changed the name of the game from Black Raven (which immediately conjures the image of a battlefield strewn with the recently eyeless dead) to Magpie, a bird much closer to their own hearts.

Unless you have years of practice behind you, it is unwise to play Magpie against a leprechaun. He will usually let you win the first couple of rounds, raising the stake each time, and then take you for all you are worth. But if you were to win the crucial round of course, you would be able to name your prize. So for those brave or reckless enough to fancy their luck, we present at the end of this book a playable example of the game, so you can get in some practice.

Music

Like all faery folk, leprechauns are wonderfully musical and are in fact responsible for some of the most famous Irish folk tunes. Many a musician has woken in the morning with a lilting melody dancing in his mind, thanks to the whistling of a leprechaun passing by in the night.

Leprechauns can play almost any instrument including, of course, the Irish harp, one of the simplest seeming of instruments, but also the hardest to play well. It was the invention of the Tuatha de Danann way back in the days of their glory. The Gael gladly took it over and at one time master harpers were the only musicians allowed to sit at the king's table during a feast, such was the honour of the calling.

Leprechauns were also quick to master the instrument for their own purposes. Their music is very different from that of the Tuatha's descendants, the Sidhe; it has an earthy quality that speaks directly to the heart, whereas the Sidhe's music is more abstract and sounds like the chiming of stars. Merry or sad, leprechaun music has a magic ability to sound familiar and strange at the same time, and both happy and sad. If a leprechaun wants to make you dance, it is impossible to resist.

The greatest leprechaun harpers and musicians generally come from Munster province in the south west of Ireland. The greatest lyric writers come from Ulster in the north, with the result that often leprechaun tunes have no words till they drift to Ulster, and poems have no tune till they drift south. Or sometimes the two come together at the great Beltane Fair at Uisnech.

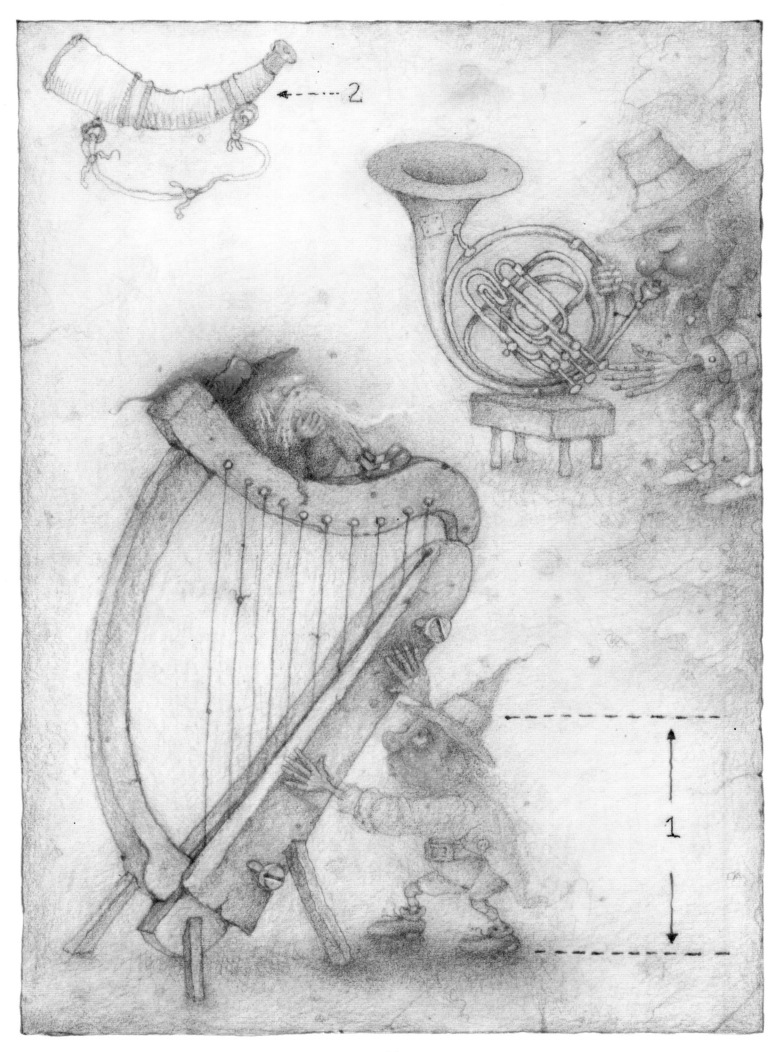

Ogham

BEFORE THE COMING OF CHRISTIANITY TO IRELAND, THERE WAS a great taboo against writing down most forms of knowledge, so bards and druids and the like committed the whole of their history and beliefs to memory. This was not because they lacked writing but because they believed timing and circumstance were as essential to understanding as words in themselves. If they did wish to write things down, usually for purely practical purposes, they used Greek or Roman letters, or else their own secret script, Ogham. This was said to have been invented by one of the Tuatha, Ogma Sun Face, who carved the characters on the four edges of a stone pillar he erected for the purpose.

There were twenty characters in the original Ogham alphabet, divided into four groups of five, each character made of up to five straight lines. These were carved along the corner of a pillar or wooden stave and read from bottom to top, or from left to right. On a flat surface the corner was marked by a line running through the middle of the characters. Later five more symbols were invented to convey new sounds that came into the tongue, but Ogma had little to do with these and they were in fact very rarely used, except maybe for ritual or divinatory purposes. The original alphabet was easily adapted into a sign language that druids and bards used to communicate secretly between themselves in unlettered company. Or possibly the sign language came first.

Some books are said to have been written by the bards and druids towards the end of their ascendance, carved in Ogham on hundreds of staves of wood, but if so none has survived. Ogham was also used in a complicated form of mysticism relating the letters of the alphabet to sacred trees and a multitude of other things; but its most common use that has left any trace is on memorials and place markers. That is how leprechauns use Ogham today, only they rarely carve the letters into stone or wood any more. Their messages are traced with what we call magic and are only visible by moonlight, shining like silver; and then only to those gifted with the Sight, or having a stone with a natural hole bored through it, or some other such charm.

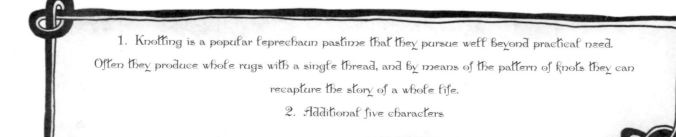

1. Knotting is a popular leprechaun pastime that they pursue well beyond practical need. Often they produce whole rugs with a single thread, and by means of the pattern of knots they can recapture the story of a whole life.
2. Additional five characters

OGHAM.

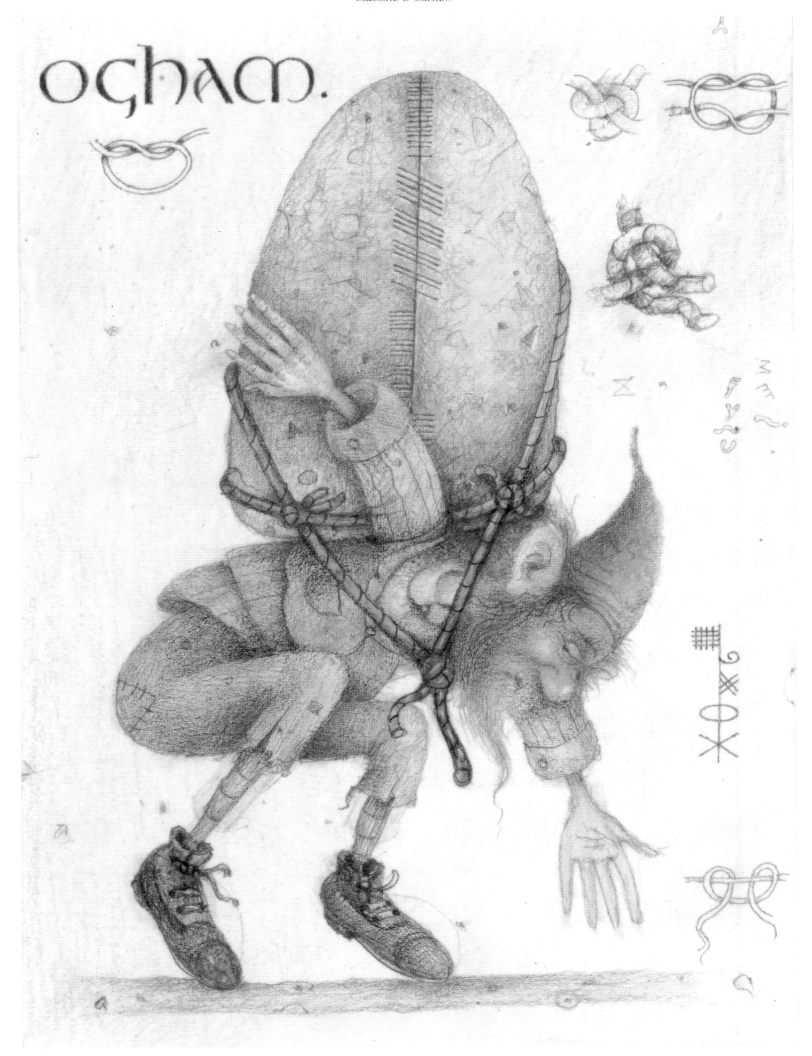

Leprechauns & Magic

LTHOUGH AN EARTHY PEOPLE, leprechauns are still faeries and have a famous command of magic. But to them it is not seen as magic but the simple operation of natural laws. It is a source of continual wonder to leprechauns that we cannot see or do half the things they can, while in other ways they cannot help admiring and emulating us.

Rainbows

VERYONE HAS HEARD THAT WHERE a rainbow touches the ground you will find buried treasure. Not many people seriously believe this any more, and science suggests that there is no such spot anyway – where a rainbow appears to touch ground is completely dependent on where you are standing, so will be different for each observer. Leprechauns don't dispute this but say it is missing the point. Which is that in chasing rainbows what matters as much as anything is knowing when you are at the right spot from which to view the rainbow. Then if you determine where it ends, you will pinpoint the treasure. It depends as much on knowing where you are coming from as where you are going to, which requires a particular kind of instinct.

Not many humans have it, so for most of us chasing rainbows is a pretty pointless activity; but leprechauns, being that much more in tune with the hidden currents of destiny and time and all that kind of thing, are quite often successful. And the advantage of rainbow chasing is that it is a solitary activity, which means the gold does not have to be shared out at the end.

Leprechauns also often use rainbows to mark where they have buried their own treasure, scrambling the signals so that other leprechauns cannot unravel the secret. The treasure they do find is therefore nearly always that buried by humans long ago. Of which there is no shortage in Ireland, where there is still far more treasure beneath the ground than in all the museums of the world. Anyone wishing to bury a treasure and not have it taken by leprechauns is advised to plant a hawthorn or whitethorn bush over it. This places the treasure under their protection and they are bound by their own laws to guard it against your return.

Lunar rainbows, because of their rarity, mark the greatest treasures of all, those that lie waiting still to astonish the world with their glimpse of Erin in the days of her glory.

Opposite; Note that leprechauns use the wishbone of a chicken when dowsing for gold. This is the origin of the superstition about wishbones among humans. The seat of this ingenious leprechaun's cycle can be raised and lowered according to the terrain he is in.

Leisure

One of the perils of fishing, leprechauns find, is that of catching something larger than themselves. However, looked at another way, this also adds to the excitement.

Leprechauns are by nature a hard-working race but like everyone they take a break to refresh themselves occasionally. Often they go treasure hunting, which to them is as much a leisure activity as it is work, but fishing has a similar appeal for the stomach. If they are desperately hungry, leprechauns are quite able to make fish jump out of a stream into their frying pans, but this is seen as an abuse of their powers so they generally use more down-to-earth methods.

Mortality

Leprechauns live to an immense age, a thousand or two years is no big deal, but they are no more immortal than you or me and people have occasionally witnessed leprechaun funerals. You would of course find no remains in the ground were you to be so unfeeling as to dig up the grave. Leprechauns have skeletons just like us, but they only half exist in our world, so when they die their mortal remains slip wholly into the faery dimension.

It was once commonly believed that leprechauns, like some other faeries, exchanged elderly and infirm members of their own race for human babies, so they would be cared for. Mothers would find their babies strangely changed overnight into wizened creatures with strange, un-babylike habits. There were ways of testing if it was a changeling. One was to leave bagpipes or some other musical instrument by the crib and pretend to leave the house. Then if it was a changeling, wonderful music would soon be heard, because it would be unable to resist playing the instrument.

Or the changeling could be tricked into talking and revealing its age. Eggshells were a favourite means of tricking the creature (they are natural hiding places for faeries in human homes, so they have a special interest in them). The mother would carefully crack the eggs, throw away the yolks and boil the shells up in a pot. The changeling would be so puzzled it was sure to say something like: 'In all my fifteen hundred years I never saw eggshell stew before!'

Or the people of the house would start talking of events that happened generations before, but deliberately get the stories wrong until the changeling was provoked into correcting them. As soon as its secret was out, the changeling would disappear and the baby appear in its place, or be found nearby.

Next on the list was to place the baby in a circle of fire. And if this provoked no response, you would discuss throwing it into the hearth or running a red hot poker down its throat. Any normal baby would of course not understand what you were saying, but a changeling would crack and either run away or simply disappear, leaving the true baby in its place.

How true any of this is of leprechauns is uncertain. Leprechauns themselves say it is only malignant faery folk like the fir dearg who have ever gone in for changelings, and since leprechauns are naturally honest this must be respected. What it probably means is that it has never been the general practice of leprechauns to steal human babies, so if it has happened at all it was by rogue leprechauns or other sprites which people have mistaken for leprechauns.

Chapter Three
Leprechaun Clans

BACK AT THE DAWN OF HISTORY, when the first people came to Ireland, they divided it between them into north and south halves. Then later these halves were divided again, and these divisions have broadly continued into modern times as the four main provinces of Ireland – Leinster, Munster, Connaught and Ulster. Then from each of these provinces was taken a small part and these were welded together to make the province of Meath at the centre. This was the smallest province, but it belonged to the High King of all Ireland, who had authority over all the rest.

This division of the land has remained ever since and has shaped the character of Ireland's people, including leprechauns, though leprechauns are not known to have taken much part in any of the wars that came from the division.

Generally speaking, leprechauns are too unpolitical to get involved in wars. They have clans and regional identities, rivalries and so on, but almost no hierarchical structure that might translate these into power struggles beyond the occasional scuffle or hurling match that gets out of control. They do not have kings and queens amongst themselves, except as a kind of game occasionally. Leprechauns accept the sovereignty of the Sidhe, the larger faery-folk descended from the Tuatha, and will treat a king or queen of the Sidhe with due respect, but that is about as far as it goes.

Human equivalents can expect no special treatment. If anything the reverse. Any human with too high an opinion of him- or herself can expect to have it severely tested if they meet a leprechaun.

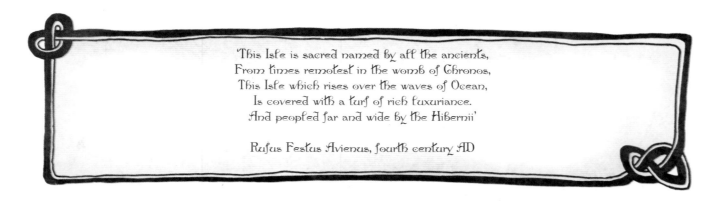

'This Isle is sacred named by all the ancients,
From times remotest in the womb of Chronos,
This Isle which rises over the waves of Ocean,
Is covered with a turf of rich luxuriance.
And peopled far and wide by the Hibernii'

Rufus Festus Avienus, fourth century AD

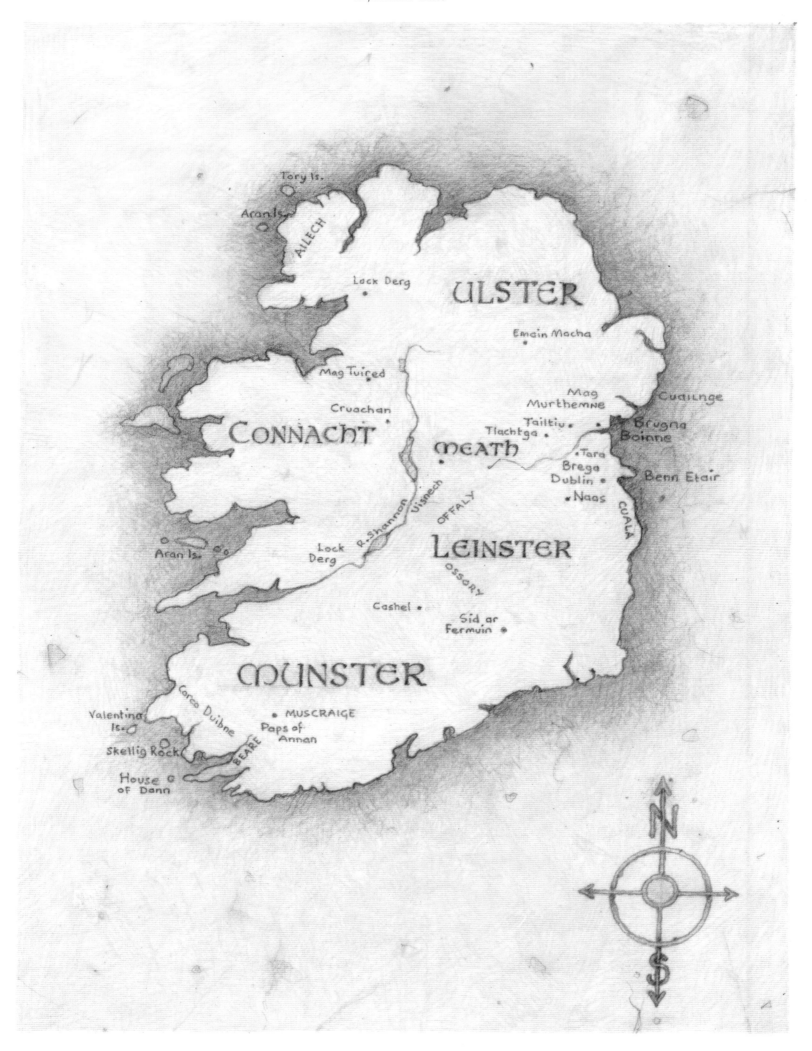

FOR SIMPLICITY WE HAVE DIVIDED the leprechauns into clans according to the provinces. Within each province there are further complex subdivisions according to kinship and district, too little is known to outsiders to unravel them meaningfully. It is worth bearing in mind that these are broad generalizations that do not necessarily apply to any particular leprechaun you may encounter. There have been great poets from Munster and great musicians from Ulster, for instance, but these are the general characteristics (or prejudices) that leprechauns hold about each other.

1. Connaught leprechauns, in their reputation at least, are said to be sober, industrious and the greatest scholars in the land, the greatest philosophers and inventors too. They are also the most reclusive and this is perhaps why we don't hear a great deal about them.

2. Ulster leprechauns, or logherymen, are said to be the best poets, though a wee bit argumentative about it. The best leprechaun boxers come from Ulster, and the best hurlers (this is in contrast with humans, whose best teams come from Tipperary and Kilkenny). Their success at these sports is slightly strange because logherymen tend to be smaller than other leprechauns, but perhaps they just work harder at them. Logherymen often wear pointed hats, on which they will sometimes invert themselves and spin like a top, usually when celebrating some particularly successful prank.

3. Meath leprechauns prize diplomacy above all other arts, even eloquence. This is because they get the most visitors from other parts and spend much of

their time mediating disputes between them. However, it is not just sweet talk they use. The leprechauns of Meath have a diplomatic technique they call 'active diplomacy'. This often involves wading into an argument and knocking the disputants' heads together till they see sense, or threatening to cut their throats if they won't reach agreement. Afterwards they will be given mead to toast their new friendship, and as the finest leprechaun mead comes from Meath this is a fair incentive in itself.

4. Leinster leprechauns probably come closest to the popular conception of leprechauns. They are the least adventurous in their dress, so will often be met wearing exactly what you would expect – the green suit and hat, the wide belt and buckle and the stout boots. They also tend to be the most prosperous and placid of leprechauns, but that makes them no less canny in avoiding handing over any of their gold to you. Honey is their favourite delicacy and because of this they have a love-hate relationship with bees (that is to say, they love bees for their honey and the bees hate them for purloining it).

5. Munster leprechauns are commonly known as cluricaunes and probably have the most distinct character of all leprechauns, though most of what is said about them is not really very complimentary. They are said to be great drinkers and wild revellers, but it must be remembered that this has probably been exaggerated by both humans and leprechauns elsewhere. What certainly is true is that there are more tales of the cluricaune behaving badly than there are of him being just like other leprechauns. But this could well just be prejudice showing itself. By way of compensation, Munster leprechauns are renowned as the finest musicians in Ireland and the sweetest talkers. When not behaving wildly they can charm the birds from the trees.

To illustrate the diversity of leprechaun lore there follows a selection of tales from each of the provinces of Ireland:

Leinster

Leprechauns are generally met alone, but not always. Thomas Keightley, one of the great gatherers of Irish folklore in the early nineteenth century, published this tale exactly as he heard it from his sister (Mrs L.), who had no reason to believe her sources were having her on:

'And usedn't people to see leprechauns in them days, mother?' said Mickey, laughing.

'Hold your tongue, you saucy cub, you,' cried Molly; 'what do you know about them?'

'Leprechauns?' said Mrs L., gladly catching at the opportunity. 'Did people really, Molly, see leprechauns in your young days?'

'Yes, indeed, ma'am; some people say they did,' replied Molly, very composedly.

'Oh come now, mother,' cried Mickey, 'don't think to be going it upon us that way; you know you seen them one time yourself, and you had not the gumption in you to catch them, and get their crocks of gold from them.'

'Now, Molly, is that really true that you saw the leprechauns?'

''Deed, and I did, ma'am; but this boy's always laughing at me about them, and that makes me rather shy of talking of them.'

'Well, Molly, I won't laugh at you; so, come, tell me how you saw them.'

'Well, ma'am, you see it was when I was just about the age of Mary, there. I was coming home late one Monday evening from the market; for my aunt Kitty, God be merciful to her, kept me to take a cup of tea. It was in the summertime you see, ma'am, much about the middle of June, and it was through the fields I came.

Well, ma'am, as I said, it was late in the evening, the sun was near going down, and the light straight in my eyes, and I came along through the bogmeadow; for it was shortly after I married to him that's gone, and we were living in this very house that you're now in; and then when I came to the castle-field – the pathway you know, ma'am, goes right through the middle of it – and it was then as fine a field of wheat as you'd wish to look at; and it was a pretty sight to see it waving so beautifully with every air of wind that was going over it, dancing to the music of a thrush, that was singing down below in the hedge. Well, ma'am, I crossed over the style that's there yet, and went along fair and easy, till I was near the middle of the field, when something made me cast my eyes to the ground, a little before me; and then I saw, as sure as I'm sitting here, no less nor three of the leprechauns, bundled together like so many tailors, in the middle of the path before me.

They were not hammering their pumps, or making any kind of noise whatever; but there they were, the three little fellows, with their cocked hats upon them, and their legs gothered up under them, working at their trade as hard as may be. If you were only to see, ma'am, how fast their little elbows went as they pulled out their ends! Well, every one of them had his eye cocked upon me, their eyes as bright as the eye of a frog, and I could not stir one step from the spot for the life of me. So I turned my head round, and prayed to the Lord in his mercy to deliver me from them. When I went to look at them again, not a sight of them was to be seen: they were gone like a dream.'
'But, Molly, why did you not catch them?'
'I was afeard, ma'am, that's the truth of it; but maybe I was as well without them. I never heard tell of a leprechaun yet that was not too many for any one that cotch him.'

NAGGENEEN

Munster

The cluricaunes of south west Ireland are famous drunkards. At least that is what the other leprechauns say of them, and whether true or not there are many tales that tell of them behaving in a wild and drunken way. Many a rich Cork and Kerry family is said to have endured cluricaune raids on their cellars.
There is the famous case of Justin MacCarthy of Ballinacarthy, a great host whose cellar shamed every other in the province. But he could not keep a butler because of the leprechaun Naggeneen, who inhabited his cellar and delighted in scaring the life out of the servants. Only to the master himself was the leprechaun reasonably civil.

It got so bad poor Justin considered moving, but Naggeneen threatened to follow wherever he went. So Justin MacCarthy had to make the best of things and fetch the wine himself for the rest of his days. And when he did die, the cluricaune had a hard time of it because the cellar was almost bare and no new tenant came along rich enough to restock it.

There is also the cautionary tale (as true as the day is long) of young Billy MacDaniel of Cork. He was a lovely lad, if a bit more fond of his drink than he was of paying for it. One bright moonlit night soon after Christmas, with the frost sparkling in the trees, Billy was weaving his way home from a cheerful time out with friends, especially cheerful as it had not cost him a penny, when he met a little man no taller than his knee. Billy guessed it was a cluricaune by the size of him and his old-fashioned dress, but he could not bring himself to refuse when the little man offered him a glass of whiskey half as big as himself.

Billy should have known better. And he did, as it happens. He well remembered his mother warning him against taking gifts from the Little People. But the thirst was on him and the chill in his bones, and the whiskey looked so clear and inviting that he accepted and downed it in one gulp. Then the little man said, 'Now don't think to cheat me as you have all the others, Billy. Out with your purse and pay me like a gentleman.'

'Pay you, is it?' replied Billy. 'Could I not just pick you up and put you in my pocket as easy as a blackberry?'

'Billy MacDaniel,' declared the little man angrily. 'You will be my servant for seven years and a day, and that is how I will be paid; so make ready to follow me.'

Billy found himself unable to resist the leprechaun's every command, so all that night was obliged to chase after him through bog and brake, over hedge and ditch without rest till dawn came. Then the cluricaune let him go, but made Billy promise to meet him again that night in the fort-field near his home.

Billy dared not refuse so that night at the fort-field he met the cluricaune again.

'Billy, I want to make a long journey tonight so saddle one of my horses for me, and another for yourself, because you must be tired after last night.'

Billy looked round and could see nothing under the moon but the mound of the old fort, a thorn tree and a stream running through a bog at the foot of the slope.

'Go to the bog' said the little man, 'and bring two of the strongest rushes you can find.'

So Billy did this and the little man ordered him to straddle one of the rushes as if it were a horse. He did the same himself then cried: 'Borram! Borram! Borram!' (which in English means 'grow') and the two rushes instantly became great horses on which they galloped away across the countryside, Billy hanging on to the tail of his because he was facing the wrong way.

At last they stopped by the door of a grand house and the little man said: 'Now Billy, do as you see me do, and follow me close because since you can't tell a horse's head from its tail you may end up walking on your head.' Then he recited some very strange words which meant nothing at all to Billy, but he managed to copy them well enough and the next moment they were spirited through the keyhole, and other keyholes after that till they found themselves in a cellar stocked to the ceiling with the finest wines. The cluricaune fell to drinking as hard as he could and Billy, obedient to his command, followed the example and decided that perhaps it was not so bad a thing after all to have such a master.

And this was the pattern of the nights that followed till there was not a rich man's cellar in all Ireland they had not raided. Then one night when Billy went to get the rushes as usual, the cluricaune told him to bring a third one because they were to have company that night. Billy knew better by now than to question his master, but he couldn't help wondering who it might be and hoped it might be another servant that perhaps he could order around as well.

Off they rode with the third rush horse in tow till they came to a farm near the old castle of Carrigogunniel in County Limerick, said to have been built by Brian Boru himself. Within the farmhouse some great celebration was going on.

'Billy,' said the cluricaune suddenly, 'I will be a thousand years old tomorrow, so I think it is full time I took myself a wife. That is why we have come, for in this house, this very night, is young Darby Riley going to be married to Bridget Rooney. And as she is a tall and comely girl, and has come of decent people, I intend to marry her myself, and take her away with me.'

'And what will Darby Riley say to that?' asked Billy.

'I did not bring you to ask questions,' replied the cluricaune, and began the words that spirited them through keyholes. In they went and, without any of the company noticing, perched high in the rafters above the feast. Below them were the priest and the piper, Darby Riley, Bridget Rooney and all their families – brothers and sisters, uncles, aunts, cousins and proud parents, and many others besides. And the table groaned with food and drink enough for twice the number.

After a while it happened that the bride sneezed, and no-one thought to say 'Bless you!' as they should, because of the priest and how he should really be the first to do this. But the priest's mouth was just then full of pork, and after a moment's pause the feast went on without the blessing being said.

'Ha!' said the cluricaune happily to Billy, his eyes gleaming with a strange light, 'I have the half of her now, surely. Let her sneeze but twice more, and she is mine, in spite of priest, massbook and Darby Riley.'

A little later the fair Bridget sneezed again, but so softly that few besides the cluricaune noticed, and again no-one said 'God bless' as they should.

Billy by now was feeling very sorry for the poor girl, thinking what a terrible thing it was that so pretty a girl of nineteen, with large blue eyes, transparent skin and dimpled cheeks, should be forced to marry his master, who was as ugly as he was close to being a thousand years old. And the leering way the cluricaune looked down at her made his blood run cold.

Just then Bridget sneezed a third time and without thinking what he was doing Billy roared out: 'God save us all!'

The little man sprang up, face shining with rage and disappointment, and shrieked like a cracked bagpipe: 'I discharge you from my service, Billy MacDaniel. Take that for your wages!' And he kicked Billy so hard he fell from the rafters and landed flat in the middle of the table below.

The astonishment of the company can be imagined, but when they heard Billy's tale he was soon forgiven. Father Cooney laid down his knife and fork and speedily married the couple before more harm could come to them, and Billy MacDaniel danced and drank his fill in the celebration that followed afterwards. And that was the last he ever saw of his master.

Opposite: Being a kind of faery, leprechauns are happily immune to the perils of tobacco. Which is lucky as, almost alone of the faery people, they have a great taste for it. They are famous pipe smokers, particularly the cluricaunes of Munster. They also smoke a variety of other herbs, blending them carefully according to recipes that pass down through generations. The leprechauns' famous, legendary even, Book of Smells contains recipes for over a thousand blends, with aromas ranging from Old Shagpile (guaranteed to stun a swarm of midges at twenty paces) to Sweetpea Surprise, which can evoke the scent of a bright midsummer morning on even the most dismal winter night.

BUT NOT ALL TALES OF THE CLURICAUNE SHOW THEM AS WILD drunkards. Close on two centuries ago Molly Cogan of Kilmallock in Limerick told Thomas Crofton Croker about a cluricaune her grandfather had met, and even caught, and really it seems no different from any other leprechaun.

It happened like this: one night as he went to the stable to tend his old mare, Molly's grandfather heard something 'hammering, hammering, hammering, just for all the world like a shoemaker making a shoe, and whistling all the time the prettiest tune he ever heard in his whole life before'.

He guessed what might be making this sound and, remembering tales of cluricaunes and their gold, he crept in. He looked around but 'never a bit of the little man could he see anywhere, but he heard him hammering and whistling and so he looked and looked, till at last did he see the little fellow; and where was he, do you think, but in the girth under the mare, and there he was with his little bit of an apron on him, and a hammer in his hand, and he was so busy with his work, and he was hammering and whistling so loud, that he never minded my grandfather till he caught the leprechaun fast in his hand.

'"Faith I have you now," says he, "and I'll never let you go till I get your purse, that's what I won't. So give it here to me at once now."

'"Stop, stop," cries the cluricaune. "Stop till I get it for you!"

So my grandfather, like a fool you see, opened his hand a little and the little fellow jumped away laughing. And he never saw him any more, and never a bit of the purse did he get, only the cluricaune left his little shoe that he was making, and my grandfather was mad enough angry with himself for letting him go; but he had the shoe all his life. And my own mother told me she often saw it, and had it in her hand, and 'twas the prettiest little shoe she ever saw. It was lost long afore I was born; but my mother told me about it often and often enough.'

Such shoes were once common heirlooms in Ireland, a great deal more common than tales of people who had any luck in getting gold from a leprechaun.

Connaught

Leprechauns usually manage to trick their way out of surrendering their gold, but not always. Lady Jane Wilde, great Irish scholar that she was (and mother of the incomparable Oscar), heard about a rich family living in her day near Castlerea in Roscommon who openly credited the origins of their fortune to a friendly leprechaun. Their story was this:

The founder of their wealth started out as a poor boy who drove a turf cart for his living. And a bare living it was too because he was not popular and people avoided having dealings with him if they could. They said he was a faery changeling because he hardly ever spoke and never joined any fun that was going. Instead he spent all his spare time reading books he had picked up on his travels. His great wish was to get rich enough to give up the cart and settle down in some pleasant house where he could devote himself to study.

Well, in his books he learned all about leprechauns and how they know the secret places where treasure is buried, and this seemed to him the most promising way by which he might fulfil his dream. So everywhere he travelled he listened out for the tap of the leprechaun's hammer, and kept his eye on every hedge for sight of the little fellow.

This made him seem stranger than ever of course to his fellow men, but at last one evening as the sun was setting he was rewarded by the sight of a little leprechaun sitting under a dock leaf and hammering away at his last, dressed all in green and with a little cocked hat on his head. Down jumped the boy from his cart and grabbed the little fellow before he could so much as twitch.

'Now I have you,' he cried, 'and you'll not be free till you tell me where to find the hidden gold.'

'Easy now,' said the leprechaun, 'don't hurt me and I'll tell you right enough. Mind you, I could hurt you if I chose, for I have the power. But I won't, for we are cousins once removed; and as we are near relations I'll just be good and show you the place of the secret gold that none can have save those of faery blood. Come along with me to the old fort of Lipenshaw where it lies. But be quick, for when the last glow of the sun vanishes, the gold will disappear too and you will never find it again.'

So off they drove in the cart to the old fort nearby and entered through a great door in the stone wall. The whole floor was covered with gold and silver and it seemed all the riches of the world were gathered there.

'Now take what you want,' said the leprechaun, 'but hurry, for if the door closes on you, you'll not escape for as long as you live.'

So the boy grabbed all the treasure he could hold and staggered with it out to the cart. He was just turning back for more when the door slammed like a clap of thunder and night fell. The leprechaun had

disappeared, which was a pity because the boy would have liked to thank him. He drove home and counted his treasure, and there was gold enough there for a king's ransom.

Telling no-one what had happened, he set off the next day for Dublin and put all his treasure in a bank, and from that day on he lived like a lord. He had a fine house built, with carriages and servants and a library such as had never been known before in those parts. And with all his learning he became a great and powerful man in the country, with a high reputation which his family continued after him. And they remained as rich as ever, despite giving freely to the poor. Or perhaps because of it, for often luck depends on generosity.

Connaught is the home of many great leprechaun philosophers. Here we see one testing out the story of the tortoise and the hare. To get round the problem of the hare maybe having heard the tale already, and so being on his guard, the philosopher raced them separately over the same route and timed them. The hare won anyway, of course, as would any hare outside of a moral fable.

Ulster

SOMEONE WHO TASTED THE BITTER TRUTH OF THE SAYING 'Beware what you wish for because it may come true' was Tom Pearce of Letterkenny in Donegal. Tom was an upright fellow, honest, cheerful and mostly sober. But, having no land of his own and no great skill beyond hard work to offer, he was also very poor. It was all right in summer and at harvest when every farmer in the townland welcomed an extra pair of hands. But the winters were hard.

To make matters worse, Tom had no talent for putting anything by for such times. When he had money in his pocket he spent it. When he hadn't he went hungry.

For all his friendly ways and gay humour when he was on top of the world, Tom was the despair of his wife Joaney who tried to keep their home together through all the ups and downs. Many's the winter night when he would come home from a day's fruitless trudging round the country looking for work, and they would fall to arguing.

'Joaney,' he would say, 'why is it that after the hard day I've just had, with the cold in my bones and a hole in my stomach, we have no fire to warm ourselves by? Why is there no more for my supper than a slice of old griddle bread, without even a dab of butter or a drop of sour milk to soften it?'

'Tom,' she would reply sharply, 'there's no fire because the peat's all gone and the larder's empty too. All we have to eat and burn are the stones in the yard.'

'Are you implying that it's my fault, then, Joaney?' Tom would ask in wonder, for this was a notion that always came as a surprise to him. And then the arguing would begin.

One cold winter sunset as he was heading home to just such a scene, Tom heard a curious tapping sound close by, and a cheerful whistle coming from somewhere under a hedge. As quiet as a mouse he crept up and what should he see but a little leprechaun no taller than his knee, sat cross-legged on a pile of stones and tapping away at a tiny shoe on his last.

Such a racket was the little fellow making that he never heard Tom arrive. So Tom reached out quickly and held him fast.

'Let go, let me go!' shrieked the leprechaun. 'What have I done to deserve being grabbed so rudely?'

'Nothing yet' replied Tom, 'but it's a lot I'm hoping you'll be able to do for me before I let you go. Now let's be having your magic purse that never runs short of gold.'

'Damn me, I must be getting careless,' grumbled the leprechaun. 'That's the third time this week I've been caught and they all want the same thing, me magic purse, me magic purse. I have no purse! It's been robbed from me already!'

'All right then,' said Tom, who had been taught never to soften with a leprechaun, 'then tell me where there's some treasure buried nearby.'

'Hasn't that also been taken already?' cried the leprechaun. 'I've been caught so often by lummocks like you there's no treasure left in the county.'

'What about the wishes then?' asked Tom, winking first with one eye then the other so he had one eye on the little man all the time.

The leprechaun looked cross. 'So you know about the wishes then?' he replied grumpily.

'I know all about leprechauns, me little feller,' Tom said. 'Didn't I learn it at me mammy's knee? Why d'you think I'm only blinking just the one eye at a time? Don't I know that if I take both eyes off you for a second you'll vanish?'

'All right then,' said the leprechaun at last. 'You can have the three wishes. But if you want my advice you'll think carefully before making them. It's not as simple as you think, wishing for anything in the world.'

So Tom looked thoughtfully up at the sky where the stars were just beginning to show and the moon was rising out of the clouds. And of course when he looked back he held nothing in his hand but the stump of a gorse bush.

Well, that did it for Tom Pearce. Going home to cold and famine when he had held the promise of a fortune in his hands put him in a worse mood than ever. And when he sat down again to nothing but a dry scrap of griddle bread for supper, the awfulness of it all got the better of him.

'God, woman,' he declared, 'but it's a hard life we have. How I wish we had a black pudding up before us on the table here, and it as round as the griddle that bread was baked on!'

There came a clap of thunder and a puff of smoke, and from out of nowhere appeared a steaming hot black pudding that almost broke the table with its weight. Joaney shrieked and Tom fell off his stool in surprise. Then he recalled the leprechaun, and remembered that the little man had in fact already promised him the three wishes before disappearing.

A great smile came to Tom's face when he saw that his troubles were over. But Joaney was less pleased when she had heard all his tale. 'What?' she screamed. 'You have three wishes for anything in the world and all you can think of is a great big black pudding?!'

So they fell to arguing. The argument went this way and that but always it ended in Joaney crying: 'But I can't believe that all you could think to wish for was a black pudding!'

Finally in a rage Tom yelled: 'I wish to God that this black pudding you're making such a fuss about would stick to your face and shut you up!'

No sooner said than with another clap of thunder and puff of smoke it was done. And nothing they tried could shift the black pudding from Joaney's face one bit. So in the end poor Tom Pearce had no choice but to use his last wish to free Joaney, and make the black pudding disappear.

Meath

Leprechauns usually outwit humans and see many things which we cannot, but they are not always one step ahead. From Kilberry in Meath comes the tale of Bridie O'Neill who once outsmarted a leprechaun.

It all began one evening on her way home from the bean fields where she had been working. Suddenly Bridie heard a sound like a sob from the hedge beside the road. She parted the bushes and there on a large toadstool sat a tiny man with his head in his hands looking as miserable as the day is long.

'Whatever is the matter?' she asked, so moved to pity she didn't at first think how strange the situation was.

He looked up slowly.

'How would you feel,' he asked, 'if you had just lost every precious thing you had in the world?'

By now Bridie had guessed she was addressing a leprechaun, but all notions of magic purses or crocks of gold were banished by his unhappiness.

'You poor thing,' she said, pushing in beside him. 'How did this happen?'

'It's a long story,' the little man replied.

'Well, that's all right, I'm in no rush.'

'My mistake,' he began, 'was letting that feller talk me into telling him my true name and him lying to me about his...' And he began to tell her how he had been tricked by a rogue leprechaun called Trig (not his 'true' name of course).

'And the next thing I know,' concluded the little man, 'he's taken all the treasure I own and hidden it where I can never find it.'

But Bridie told him not to be so despairing and how there must surely be some happy answer if only they could think of it. So they got to talking about ways they might get the treasure back, and in their talk it emerged that among the stolen treasure was a ring that Bridie's mother had lost years before, a wedding ring she had broken her heart over trying to find. And this made the leprechaun feel worse than ever because here was Bridie being so nice and comforting to him, and all the while he had been keeping something that rightfully belonged to her. But the ring turned out to be what made them think of a plan.

When they had worked it all out, the leprechaun gave Bridie a little jar of ointment, which she was to rub in her eyes so she could see everything a leprechaun can see, and off she set for the place where the other leprechaun Trig lived. When she got there, sure enough there he was sitting under a tree on top of a little hill.

'Good day, sir,' said Bridie politely. Trig started and was clearly not pleased that she could see him so clearly.

'Good day to you too,' he said a bit grudgingly, 'what can I do for you, young miss?'

'I've lost a ring belonging to my mother,' Bridie told him, 'and seeing a leprechaun sat there under the tree I was wondering if maybe you could help me find it. For I've heard it said that leprechauns are the greatest finders of lost rings in the world.'

Trig swelled up a little at this compliment and sat up straight. 'Have you indeed?' he said. 'And of course it is true, so describe this ring to me exactly.'

Bridie did so and after a while the leprechaun Trig said: 'Very well, wait here, I'll not be long.' And off he trotted into the trees. But what he didn't know was that Bridie's leprechaun friend was hiding in there waiting to follow and see where he had hidden the ring along with the rest of the stolen treasure. And it all worked out perfectly. Trig soon returned with Bridie's ring. She gave him a coin and kept him talking for a time, and while they were talking her friend got his gold back, and a bit more to make up for all the trouble he had been through.

So there is one instance at least of a human outwitting a leprechaun. You might even say that Bridie also gave the other one a crock of gold, because she helped him get his own back again; and you can be sure that afterwards she never wanted for the practical necessities that help make life sweet.

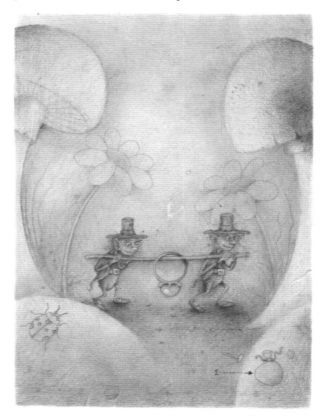

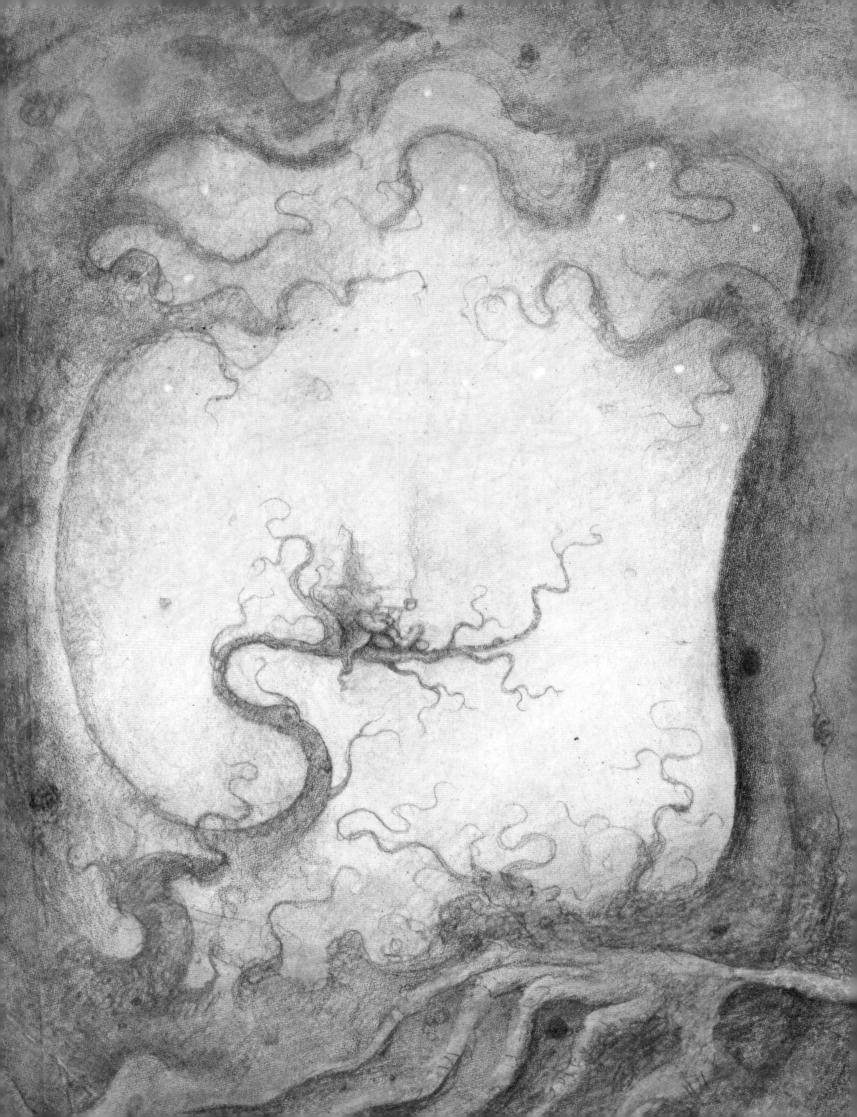

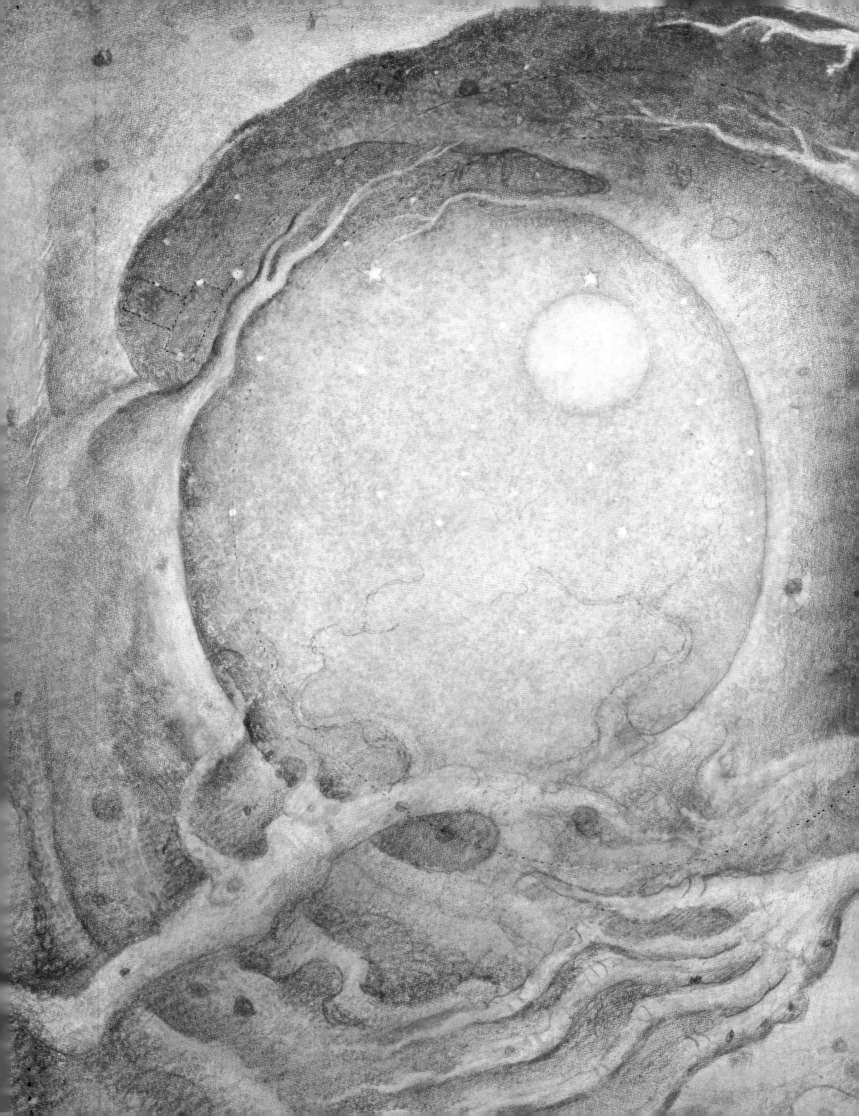

Chapter Four
Leprechaun Cousins

LEPRECHAUNS ARE JUST ONE OF hundreds of different kinds of faery people in Ireland who were once considered as much the inhabitants of the land as the Gael. Most are descended from the Tuatha de Danann who ruled Ireland before the Gael arrived. After a great battle with the Sons of Mil who came from Spain, the Tuatha withdrew into the hills and faery-forts that are gateways to the otherworld and have since played less and less of a part in the lives of humans, though Irish folklore is crowded with tales of encounters and traffic between them, marriage even. The descendants of the Tuatha are the Sidhe (pronounced Shee) who make up the bulk of faeries. They range in character from the sociable and stately Daoine Sidhe who preside over the faery kingdom, to the wailing banshee whose shrieks presage the death of notable people. In between are hordes of others both kindly and wicked, large and tiny who may be encountered still if one merely distances oneself enough from the trappings of modern life. Ben Bulben in Sligo and Slieve Gullion in Armagh are just two of many hills and mountains in Ireland of which it is said that if you spend a night alone on the summit you will return either mad or a poet (if you return at all), because you are sure to brush with the faery folk. Sceptics are recommended to try it on May Eve. Suicidal sceptics should try Halloween.

Fairies

1. It was of course the faeries who executed the finer details of great illuminated manuscripts such as the Books of Kells and Durrow, in return for which the monks granted them the honorary status of angels. This was never formally ratified by the upper echelons of the Church, though, which led to a certain bitterness among the faeries, and a falling out which meant the end of such masterpieces.

2. Winged faeries most commonly acquire their wings from insects that have died of natural causes, but occasionally they make use of flower petals.

3. Lucky shamrock. The term shamrock in fact means simply 'clover' but it has over time come to apply to just a few of the hundreds of different varieties of this and other three-leaved plants. According to the *Encyclopaedia Britannica* these include wood sorrel *(Oxalis acetosella)*, suckling clover *(Trifolium dubium)* and white clover *(Trifolium repens)*. White clover is championed by many who believe there is an 'original shamrock', but wood sorrel is the shamrock exported in vast quantities around the world from Ireland for St Patrick's Day.

It is commonly said that the shamrock became a symbol of Ireland when St Patrick used it to illustrate to the natives the nature of the Holy Trinity. Well, maybe that is true, but perhaps also the natives were just too polite to point out to him that most pagan Irish goddesses were members of trinities, so they were already very familiar with the concept. And the shamrock had long been considered a peculiarly lucky plant by the druids. When it has a fourth leaf this luck is magnified a hundred-fold.

Besides the Sidhe there are what are often called the Elementals who are faery folk or sprites associated with one or other of the prime elements of ancient philosophy – earth, air, water and fire. Leprechauns are Earth sprites, along with gnomes, dwarfs, trolls and the like. Air sprites include the winged faeries which are what most people first think of at mention of the word 'faery'. They are not necessarily winged, though it is something they affect if they feel like it.

Among air sprites the closest relation of the leprechaun is the ganconer or gancanaugh, who is a bit of a charmer and enjoys flirting with human maids. The rumour that the girls later always die of heartbreak when he abandons them is a cruel exaggeration, but it is true that 'marriage' and 'long-term relationship' are not words in his vocabulary.

ER-PEOPLE ARE AS COMMON around the coasts of Ireland as in any part of the world's oceans, and they have as much variety as the other fey folk. There are suboceanic gods like Manannan Mac Lir and his retinue, there are those who match perfectly the popular image of mermaids and men, there are merrows who are very similar but live in airy palaces beneath the waves, and then there are the water sprites who are the marine counterparts of leprechauns.

The distinction between sprites and the larger mer-people is a bit blurred; but it would seem they are closer to 'common' mermaids than to merrows, who need a red feathered cap to swim between their underwater realm and ours. If a human steals this cap the merrow is unable to get home, and this is how men have from time to time obtained for themselves merrow wives. In the last century a woman near Bantry Bay whose skin was covered in fish-like scales was said to have been descended from such a union.

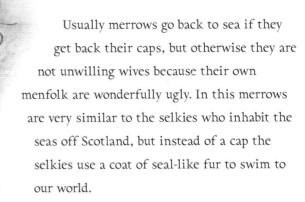

Usually merrows go back to sea if they get back their caps, but otherwise they are not unwilling wives because their own menfolk are wonderfully ugly. In this merrows are very similar to the selkies who inhabit the seas off Scotland, but instead of a cap the selkies use a coat of seal-like fur to swim to our world.

Water sprites wear headgear purely for decoration. They are great friends with coastal leprechauns and often visit them in the form of tiny 'red' cattle with no horns. As with all faery folk, nights of the full moon are when they are most likely to be spotted on the beach.

Fire sprites are extremely rare and there is no clear information about them. Some say the only fire sprites are salamanders because faeries are allergic to fire, and certainly it is true that all the other faeries are afraid of fire; but it is hard to believe, given the natural symmetry of things, that there are no other sprites specially adapted to this element.

Besides these there are other Little People in Ireland who are often confused with leprechauns and may well in fact be rogue leprechauns that have simply grown away from the rest in habit and temperament. Of particular note are the fir dearg and the phouka.

Fir Dearg

The fir dearg or fear darrig (the 'red men') are a wholly mischievous race who dress all in red and often have red hair too. Their sole interest in life seems to be playing gruesome practical jokes on humans and they have no noticeable saving graces. Luckily they are rare.

Phouka

ANY AUTHORITIES SAY THAT the *phouka*, or *pooka*, is a particularly wild and mischievous cousin of the leprechaun, which usually adopts the shape of an animal to play its wild pranks. Some have even equated it to the devil, but Lady Wilde heard a very different account. 'The phouka,' she wrote in *Ancient Legends of Ireland*, 'is a friendly being, and often helps the farmer at his work if he is treated well and kindly.'

She illustrated this with the tale of a miller's son named Phadrig who was out minding cattle one day when a strange wind passed by. Guessing what it might be, he ran after it shouting: 'Phouka, phouka! show me yourself, and I'll give you my big coat to keep you warm.' In the next field he ran into an angry bullock, but it calmed down when he threw his coat over its head and then told him (for it was of course the phouka in disguise) to go to the mill that night when the moon arose and he would find good luck.

Well Phadrig did this and saw nothing but the sacks of corn ready for grinding the next day, and the miller's men all lying asleep on the sacks. Soon he fell asleep too, but when he woke in the morning he found that all the corn had been ground, though the men were all still snoring.

This happened for three nights in a row with no clue as to who was doing the work. On the fourth night Phadrig hid himself in an old chest, determined to keep awake and watch what happened through the keyhole. At midnight he saw six little men come in, each carrying a sack of corn. The seventh was an ancient raggedy little fellow who ordered the rest about till soon the corn was all ground to flour.

The next night the miller himself came to watch from inside the trunk, and was so delighted by what he saw that he sacked all his men on the spot and was soon growing rich on the wages he no longer had to pay them. And not a word did he say to anyone about the phouka, for fear of spoiling his luck.

This went on for quite a while and Phadrig often used to hide in the trunk to watch the phouka and his fellows at work. Then at last he began to feel a bit sorry for the old fellow who, for all his labours, was still dressed like a vagrant while Phadrig and his dad were piling up the money. So Phadrig had a little suit made of the finest wool and silk and laid it out on the floor one night where the old phouka always stood to direct the operations. Then he crept into the chest to watch what followed

'How is this?' cried the phouka when he saw the suit. 'Are these for me? I shall be turned into a fine gentleman.'

So he put the clothes on and strolled up and down admiring himself. Then he remembered the milling and was about to start ordering the others about, when he stopped and cried: 'No, no. No more work for me. Fine gentlemen like myself don't grind corn.

I'll go out and see a little of the world and show off my fine clothes.' And he kicked away his old rags into a corner, and left.

So no corn was ground that night, or ever again by him and his little band of helpers, who all ran off. And Phadrig never saw his little benefactor again. However, things were not so bad. The miller sold the mill and with all the money they now had they lived the life of leisured gentlemen. Phadrig became a great scholar also and in time married a wife so beautiful people said she must be a faery princess.

But a strange thing happened at the wedding. When they stood up to toast the bride's health, Phadrig found by his hand a golden cup filled with wine. No-one knew where it had come from, but Phadrig guessed it was the phouka's gift. So he toasted his bride with it, and it must have brought

luck for they were happy and prosperous ever after. And the cup is still in the keeping of their descendants to this day.

Lady Wilde's phouka seems very much like a domesticated leprechaun, or a brownie from across the water; and perhaps this is right because 'phouka' or 'pucca' has often been linked with the English 'Puck', who may have a reputation for mischief but not wickedness. So in the wilder tales of the phouka the chances are that there has been a mingling of two quite separate traditions about quite separate beings.

The way a gift of clothes brought an end to the contract is very much what happens with the brownie in Scotland. Explanations vary as to why this is so but it happens so often that it is an integral part of the lore.

W. B. Yeats collected the tale of the Kildare pooka which, in the form of an ass, did all the housework for a friend of the storyteller. Night after night this went on till a servant of the house plucked up the courage to question him. The pooka explained that in a past life he too had been a servant in the house; an extremely lazy servant. So lazy in fact that after he died he was condemned to come back in this form and do all the chores he had not done in his life. The worst of it was, though, that having the form of an ass meant he was also condemned to spend most of his time out of doors in all weathers, and just then it was freezing winter.

The servants of the house took pity on him when they learned this, and from gratitude for all the work he was saving them, made him a fine coat. The pooka was delighted, but then revealed the end of his story, that he had been condemned to do the chores until shown a sign of gratitude. So now he was free, and that was the last they saw of him.

But again, whether this was a true pooka is debatable because although it is often said that faeries are a kind of ghost, this is a kind of Christian apology that tries to avoid the more complicated issue of where faeries fit into the scheme of things if they are not simply angels or devils.

Brownies

BROWNIES ARE CLOSE COUSINS OF THE IRISH LEPRECHAUN AND there have been many marriages between them. In fact when leprechauns cross the Irish Sea, which they have done in great numbers from time to time, they become indistinguishable from brownies after a generation or two.

Brownies are scattered throughout the Highlands and Lowlands of Scotland, and the northern counties of England. They are generally about half a yard tall, with brown, wizened faces and long, shaggy hair that grows all over their bodies; so shaggy that often they don't trouble themselves with clothes. When they do, their garments are usually brown and ragged; but it is a mistake to pity them on this account. If presented with a bright new set of clothes a brownie will generally take umbrage and leave the household. They dress the way they do because it suits them, and they hate to feel that anyone is taking pity on them. When they do accept gifts, they like to feel it is because they have earned them.

At one time most houses in Scotland had a brownie or brunaidh, who would do little jobs around the house or farm at night in return for modest gifts of food or drink. Again, these gifts must be tactfully presented by being left discreetly in the brownie's favourite place. If it seems like charity, the brownie will leave. They are particularly fond of honey and cream and fresh baked cakes, but are happy with simpler fare such as bread and milk, according to the family's circumstances. In the days when most households brewed their own beer, they would be sure to pour a little malt each time into the hollow of a stone known as the browney's stane, so he would watch over the brew and hurry it along. If this was forgotten, the chances were that the beer would go sour.

Apart from doing all the odd unfinished jobs around a house or farm, rounding up stray hens, finishing off the threshing and plaguing lazy servants in the night, a contented brownie brings good luck, without which talent and hard work count for little. If happy, the brownie will often move with the family to a new place, riding in a milk churn or some such hiding place and then running on ahead at the end to make the new domicile warm and welcoming. If offended they can ruin a family because a brownie can easily turn into a boggart or bogan, who does nothing but break things and make trouble.

BROWNIE.

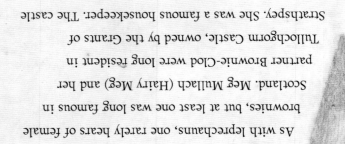

Like most faery folk, brownies hate the light of electric lamps, which are probably more responsible than anything else for their rarity these days. When they can find no congenial,

human house to live in, brownies choose caves, hollow trees or river banks as homes.

As with leprechauns, one rarely hears of female brownies, but at least one was long famous in Scotland. Meg Mullach (Hairy Meg) and her partner Brownie-Clod were long resident in Tullochgorm Castle, owned by the Grants of Strathspey. She was a famous housekeeper. The castle

was kept spotless and any dish a guest asked for was conjured as if by magic. Meg was also a great fortune teller, and a great chess player. She used to stand behind her lord's

chair during a game and silently steer him to victory.

Somehow Meg fell out with the Grants and moved away. Thereafter she travelled round Scotland not usually stopping long, apart from a while at the mill in Fincastle in Perthshire. Her temper became dangerous, though, and she seems to have turned into a boggart.

BOGGART.

A True Tale

CALLUM MOR MACINTOSH WAS A CROFTER LIVING NEAR Lochaber around the time of the Highland clearances. He had a brownie living with him with whom he was sometimes at war and sometimes quite friendly. One day for instance the brownie jumped out on Callum as he was coming home from market. Callum fought him off and carried on home, but when he arrived he found he had lost his best handkerchief, the one specially blessed for him by the priest. So Callum went looking and found the brownie rubbing the handkerchief on a rough stone.

'It's as well you came looking, Callum,' said the brownie, 'for if I'd rubbed a hole in this it would've been the death of you. And you'll still have to fight me for it.'

So they fell to fighting again and Callum got his handkerchief back. But then shortly after, when Callum was snowed in and unable to get to a birch tree he had felled for the stove, he heard a loud thud outside and found the brownie had dragged it there for him. Then later when he moved house, the brownie brought along a cart he had left behind, saving Callum a ten-mile journey.

Later still when Callum was forced to move to America, he found the brownie waiting for him in the form of a goat. 'Ha, ha! Callum,' he said, 'I'm here before you.'

REDCAP.

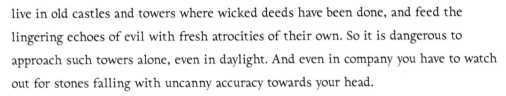

REDCAPS ARE among the most vicious of the leprechaun's Scottish cousins. At first sight they can look quite similar to brownies and the like, but the red in their caps comes not from vegetable dye but the blood of passing strangers they have stoned to death. Redcaps live in old castles and towers where wicked deeds have been done, and feed the lingering echoes of evil with fresh atrocities of their own. So it is dangerous to approach such towers alone, even in daylight. And even in company you have to watch out for stones falling with uncanny accuracy towards your head.

Human strength counts for nothing against redcaps but they can be driven off with quotes from scripture or a crucifix. They are also known as redcombs, bloody caps, dunters or powries, and you need most beware when their caps are looking dull because it means they are on the lookout for fresh blood to smarten them up.

Bwca

The Welsh bwca is a close relation of the brownie, and can also be very helpful round the home. He is more particular than the brownie about cleanliness and neatness though, and will do no work at all if the place is too untidy to start with. Bwca need to be treated with the utmost respect because if they take offence they can become regular demons, throwing things around the house at night, spoiling the milk and the baking and ruining the beer. There is no end to the mischief of an offended bwca in fact, they are as dreadful enemies as they are good friends. The only solution if you have fallen out with your bwca is to call in someone who knows how to drive him away for good.

Bwca are said to despise teetotallers and dissenting ministers, which in the past kept them rather busy in Wales.

BUCA.

Piskies

CORNISH PISKIES (PIXIES, PIGSIES) are the closest to leprechauns of all their British cousins, in behaviour anyway. They are generally portrayed rather differently as slim, almost naked elfs, wearing ragged green clothes and pointed red hats. They have pointed ears and chins and turned-up noses. Often they appear cross-eyed, but this is probably just some kind of insult to humans. There are conflicting accounts of their origins. Some suggest a faery origin as field sprites, which is true for genuine piskies, while others say they are unbaptised souls neither good enough for heaven — or bad enough for hell. As we mentioned before, this is probably a Christian rationalization.

Piskies are said to have been originally as large as humans, but to have steadily dwindled in stature down the ages. Most are now only about a foot tall, and some are no larger than ants. For this reason it is considered unlucky in Cornwall to harm ants, in case they are meryons, or dwindled faeries. Piskies are found throughout Cornwall, Devon and Somerset (where they are also called grigs). They are normally solitary, but occasionally gather for fairs and feasts at which they dance to the music of crickets, frogs and grasshoppers, plus their own instruments for they are as musical as all faeries.

In mischievous mood they love to lead people astray and into bogs. Being 'piskie-led' or 'piskie-mazed' was once considered a very real peril on the moors of south-west Britain, and many is the tale of hapless humans who only just escaped with their lives; and some that did not. But it is generally agreed that only the wicked need seriously fear being led astray. Often at night people will be led by a mischievous light or will-o'-the-wisp until they are hopelessly lost. Sometimes they see nothing but just find themselves going round and round the same field, unable to reach the path home even though they can see it clearly most of the time. Then they know that a piskie is misguiding their feet. The cure is to sit down and turn your stockings inside out, or sometimes just turning out your pockets will do the trick. There was a famous case of this in the parish of Costenton, or Constantine, about a hundred years ago. Not knowing the cure, the poor woman could only call out for help until someone came to her rescue.

There are many tales, too, of children being led astray, but this is usually a mark of favour. They are found unharmed with wonderful stories to tell and are noticeably lucky in later life.

Piskies also love to steal horses and ride them round in circles, which creates faery rings or 'gallitraps' of darker grass. Often as you pass one of these places you will hear faint sounds of revelry. As with leprechauns, if you then step into the ring with both feet you will become the piskies' prisoner. But if you put just one foot in, you will be able to see them without being caught.

Piskies generally live in caves, groves of trees or meadows, but they sometimes adopt a family and move in with them. Then they will help with housework, threshing and spinning and doing other such chores.

Like brownies they appreciate being repaid with tactful gifts, but are generally insulted by gifts of clothing and will move out. Bowls of fresh water or milk should be left out for them as reward, and bread or cakes.

A True Tale

Like cluricaunes in Ireland, piskies are fond of raiding the wine cellars of human gentry. From Luxulyan in Cornwall, in the bad old days when a thief was likely to end up on the gallows, comes the tale of John Sturtridge. One Christmas he was celebrating with other tin-miners, or 'streamers' in a hostelry called The Rising Sun above a moor called the Couse where they worked. They were in fact celebrating the original discovery of tin there by a man called Picrous, a festival which in those days was taken very seriously.

Well, John Sturtridge did his share of celebrating and then headed off rather unsteadily into the night for home. All went well till near Tregarden Down he came upon a group of piskies partying under a huge granite boulder. They shouted and laughed at him so John hurried on, a bit frightened. Soon he was totally lost, and soon after that he found himself back at the boulder. This time the piskies cried: 'Ho! and away for Par beach!' And for some strange reason John found himself shouting along too. In a twinkling he found himself on sandy Par beach with the piskies, and this time they let him join in their dancing and singing. Then the cry went up again: 'Ho! and away for Squire Tremain's cellar!' and they were all whisked away to Heligan and into the squire's cellars there, which were full of beer and wine and all other liquors one can think of. Now the party really began and if the truth be told, poor old John Sturtridge supped a good deal more than was good for him; and when the cry went up again: 'Ho! and away for Par beach!' he was too slow to join in and was left behind.

So morning found him there in the cellar among the spoils of the celebration feeling very much the worse for wear. Strangely enough, the butler would not believe his tale, and the squire was even less sympathetic. John Sturtridge was thrown into jail, tried and convicted of burglary. Then one morning he was led out to the gallows tree where a crowd had gathered for his execution. Well, poor John was just preparing to meet his Maker when there was a disturbance in the crowd and a little old woman forced her way to the front. In a shrill voice which he recognized, she cried: 'Ho! and away for France!' And in a flash they both disappeared, leaving the squire furious.

An old woman who lived on the moors was going home with an empty basket from market after selling her goods. Near the bridge over Blackabrook at the Ockerry a small figure leaped from the hedge and began dancing in the road before her. She recognized him for a piskie eighteen inches tall. She almost turned back for fear of enchantment and being led astray, but thinking of her family waiting, she pressed on. At the bridge the piskie turned and hopped towards her. Quickly she caught him and popped him into her basket, thinking that perhaps she would lead a piskie astray for a change. The little fellow was too cramped to struggle but he chattered away to her unintelligibly as she hurried home, bursting to show her prize to the family.

Suddenly the chattering stopped, and she thought he must be sulking or asleep. After a while she decided to peep in, but he had vanished. No harm came to her and she afterwards boasted of what she had done.

Spriggans

PISKIES IN CORNWALL ARE CLOSEST to leprechauns, but it is spriggans who guard the treasure. Spriggans are standing stone sprites said to have come over from Brittany where they are known as korreds. In fact they are said to have brought over the standing stones and set them up in Cornwall in the first place. Some say spriggans are dwindled giants. They generally look small, even tiny, but can quickly swell up to enormous size, especially when defending buried treasure. In appearance they are dour or fierce and often dreadfully ugly. They have a lot in common with Scottish boggarts except they usually content themselves with frightening people and robbing them, not actually harming them; unless one believes the rumour that it is they who blight crops and bring bad weather.

Turning your clothes, or even just a pocket, inside out is said in Cornwall to be a good charm against spriggans, or indeed any of the faery folk. Someone who put this to the test was the old widow of

Trencrom Hill, near the village of Chyanwheal. For some reason her cottage was chosen as a meeting place for spriggans and most nights they gathered there to divide their spoils, while the old woman hid under the bedclothes and pretended to be asleep. At the end they always left her a coin for payment, so in fact she did not do so badly out of it, for a miner's widow, but she was not satisfied and hatched a plan to change her life for the better once and for all.

One night when they fell to arguing over a spectacular pile of gold and jewellery, she contrived to turn her shift inside out under the bedclothes, leaped out of bed, placed her hand on the treasure and cried: 'You shan't have any of it!'

The spriggans scattered in amazement and terror at the charm, but one of them struck her in passing and, although she was indeed very rich from that day on, and moved to St Ives to live like a gentlewoman, if ever she put on that shift again she suffered agonies from it.

Knockers

KNOCKERS ARE GENERALLY HELPFUL Cornish mine sprites, and tin miners used often to hear them at work. Sceptics might say they were only hearing echoes but tin miners would often hear them already at work when they arrived, and carrying on when they left.

Often they have also been heard at work in long abandoned mines.

Knockers are naturally attracted to rich seams and following the sound of their little picks has led to many a rich strike. They also warn against cave-ins and floods by hammering wildly, appearing at the entrance to the shaft and throwing obstructions in the way of human miners. So in the days when gold and tin were seriously mined in Cornwall, the miners took care to keep in with them, leaving little gifts of food and drink and taking care not to whistle or swear when underground. Laughter and singing were permitted, however, so a happy mine was often a prosperous one.

Few miners ever actually saw the knockers but there was one, Captain Mathy, who, as an old man in the late nineteenth century, happily told of his encounter. He had been following their tapping in the hopes of striking a rich vein, when he broke into a little cavity lined with crystals. Within were three of the 'knackers': 'They were no bigger, either one of them, than a good sixpenny doll; yet in their faces, dress and movements they had the look of hearty old tinners. I took the most notice of the one in the middle. He was settan down on a stone, his jacket off and his shirt sleeves rolled up. Between his knees he held a little anvil, no more than an inch square, yet as complete as ever you seed in a smith's shop. In his left hand he held a boryer about the size of a darning-needle, which he was sharpan for one of the knackers, and the other was waitan his turn to have the pick he held in his hand new cossened, or steeled.'

When Mathy turned aside for another candle to see them better they disappeared, squeaking with laughter.

In Wales knockers are known as coblynau and seem as close in general character and habits as the Welsh are to the Cornish. Such mine sprites are known throughout Europe. In Scotland they are called black dwarfs, in Austria as shaft dwarfs and in Germany as mountain monks. Their size varies from a few inches to three feet.

COBLYNAU.

Hobgoblins

The word hobgoblin has come to mean something like 'demon', thanks to the Puritans, who had no time for any of the faeries; but it was once an affectionate term for the English cousin of the Scottish brownie and Welsh bwca. The English hobgoblin also has a variety of more familiar names such as Robin Goodfellow, Robin Roundcap, Puck, Tom-tit and Hob-thrush Hob. Hobgoblins are now very rare and, as far as humans are concerned, faded into legend long before their Celtic cousins, outside of a few rural pockets where belief lingered into the nineteenth century.

In their heyday their favourite place was by or behind the kitchen fire (hob) and once settled in, the hobgoblin would rarely leave the house. When offended or feeling neglected, one of the hobgoblin's more annoying pranks was to steal keys and hide them in the most unlikely places.

Robin Goodfellow

Among the rest was a good fellow devil,
So-called in kindness, 'cause he did no evil,
Known by the name of Robin (as we hear)
And that his eyes as big as saucers were,
Who came anights, and would make Kitchens clean
And in the bed bepinch a lazy queane*.
Was much in miffs about the grinding Meal,
(And sure I take it, taught the Miller steal,)
Amongst the cream bowls and milk pans would be,
And with the country wenches, who but he.
To wash their dishes for some fresh-cheese hire:
Or set their pots and kettles 'bout the fire.

from Rowland's *More Knaves Yet*
* servant

The most famous English hobgoblin in the sixteenth and seventeenth centuries was Robin Goodfellow. The son of Oberon and a country wench, he had a history of his own. But many of his adventures were probably first told about other sprites and his name became a nickname for hobgoblins in general. Robin was often confused with Puck, also a hobgoblin, but Shakespeare, who single-handedly preserved much English faery lore, kept them distinct.

Puck was also conceived by Oberon. His mother raised him with no knowledge of his origins, but from time to time they received gifts from the faery folk. Puck was clever and mischievous, but displayed no special faery powers till he was about six years old, when he ran away from home and had a vision of faeries in the woods. He woke to find a golden scroll from Oberon himself, conferring magic powers on him, including the granting of wishes and the power of shape-shifting. But there was a condition that he must use these powers to help the good and thwart the bad. If faithful to these conditions, said the scroll, he would at last be allowed into faeryland. So he set out on his career of pranks wherein was usually a lesson for the victim.

Kobolds

NDER A VARIETY OF NAMES SUCH helpful but mischievous Little People are known throughout Europe, and in fact much of the world. In Germany and neighbouring countries they are called kobolds. It is said they resemble very wrinkled little old men wearing pointed hoods and green clothing. In return for a little milk and scraps of food they will do any little job that needs doing around the house and barn. If neglected they can turn nasty and behave like poltergeists.

Kobolds are said to have been tree sprites originally. They were captured by cutting down the tree they inhabited and whittling it down to a little mannikin. This was shut in a box and taken home, where it would bring good luck. The kobold was also bound to go about the house at night doing little jobs. Only the kobold's master could open the box. If anyone else did, the sprite would escape and take revenge for its captivity by breaking things and playing tricks on the family. This is the origin of Jack-in-the-boxes. They were first made to warn children what would happen if they touched the kobold's box. In time kobolds found that in fact they rather enjoyed domestic life so force became unnecessary: they would adopt a family of their own accord.

Wight is a generalized term for small household sprites, including kobolds. With slight variations according to dialect and tongue the word has been used across Germany, Scandinavia, Iceland and the other Nordic islands of the North Atlantic. From there the term spread to neighbouring peoples like the Scots and English who applied it to brownies and hobgoblins, who are in fact quite happy with the term. In Scotland they are said to sing:

'If you call me blessed wight
I'll be your friend both day and night.'

So with little effort the word 'wight' includes the leprechaun and all of the cousins considered in this book, plus many others for which there was no room. If you look further abroad, what emerges is that at one time or another most people around the world have met or at least believed in races of small people living semi-visibly alongside humans, often in their very homes. Europeans found such traditions among the natives of North America when they arrived there and similar beliefs turn up in China, Australia, Africa and pretty much everywhere else. These have often led to wild anthropological theories about early pigmy inhabitants of those regions. In places like Africa, where genuine pigmy races still survive, there is even some truth to these theories, but they usually miss the point, which is that the Little People or wights are supernatural beings and are generally recognized as such by those who encounter them.

Leprechauns are just one variety. They are probably the most famous of the Little People and have a character quite distinct from even their closest relations just across the Irish Sea, but they are only as unique as the Irish people themselves. Which is to say that yes they are in many ways, and there are good reasons why leprechauns have thrived longer in Ireland than their cousins elsewhere, but they are not totally peculiar to Ireland.

One thing about leprechauns that stands them apart from brownies, kobolds and the like is their relative independence of us. Some of them like to move in with humans but most don't. They find us interesting but like to get on with their own lives.

Their fondness for gold has often been held against them, or used as an excuse for robbing leprechauns with a clear conscience. It is even quite shocking how ruthlessly some people used to talk about them a hundred or two years ago, as if they almost deserved to be robbed because they had all this treasure and did nothing with it. But there is a lesson or two to be learned from leprechauns. Their fondness for gold and other treasure may look like simple miserliness, which everyone knows is a vice; but when you think about it, it does no great harm. Leprechauns love precious things but, being earth sprites, they do not despoil the earth to get them. They live almost invisibly in the landscape and have very little personal vanity. There is much to be said for the leprechaun approach to life.

Bibliography

Allingham, William, *Irish Songs and Poems*, Reeves and Turner (London, 1887).

Arrowsmith, Nancy (with Moorse, George), *A Field Guide to the Little People*, (London 1977).

Briggs, Katharine, *A Dictionary of Fairies, Hobgoblins, Brownies, Bogies, and Other Supernatural Creatures* (London 1976). *The Fairies in Tradition and Literature*, (London 1967).

Croker, Thomas Crofton, *Faery Legends and Traditions of the South of Ireland*, (1834). Reprinted in Ireland: *Myths and Legends* (1995).

Evans-Wentz, W. Y., *The Faery Faith in Celtic Countries* (1911), Reprinted 1977.

Gregory, Lady, *Irish Myths and Legends* (1998).

Visions and Beliefs in the West of Ireland (2 vols; London 1920).

Hunt, Robert, *Popular Romances of the West of England* (1865). Reprinted 1993.

Keightley, Thomas, *The Faery Mythology* (1833). Reprinted London 1968.

O'Sullivan, Sean, *Folktales of Ireland* (London 1966).

Rhys, John, *Celtic Folklore* (Oxford 1901).

Wilde, Lady Jane Francis, *Ancient Legends of Ireland* (1887).

Yeats, William Butler (Ed.); *Faery and folk tales of the Irish Peasantry* (1888). Reprinted New York 1991.

Magpie

Alternative Opening Positions

👑 Himself (White King)   🌀 White Pieces   ◆ Red (Brown) Pieces

Playing the Game

1. The board can be found inside both covers of this book; use whichever board takes your fancy. Coins will do for counters, or pawns and a King or Queen from chess. Choose one of the alternative opening positions (above) and set out the pieces. The White King (Himself) sits at the centre surrounded by four White men.

2. The first thing to notice about the board is the five black squares. These are the King's Squares, because only Himself may occupy them. Other pieces may pass over the central square, but not stop there. These squares can also be used to capture opponents (see Capturing below).

3. The object of the game for White is simply for the King to reach one of the corner squares. It doesn't matter how many other White pieces are captured as long as he does this. Red's aim is to capture the King, or trap him so that neither he nor any of his companions can move.

4. All pieces apart from the King move like the Rook or Castle in chess. That is, they can travel as far as they like along a row or column until meeting an obstruction, but cannot change direction in mid-move or go diagonally.

5. The King moves the same way, but only one square at a time.

6. To avoid deadlocks, repetitive moves (where players just move back and forth between the same spots) are only allowed twice. On the third time, whoever started it must do something different.

7. Because the game is unbalanced (White has a slight advantage despite being outnumbered) games are played in 'rounds' or pairs, with players changing sides. A victory is only scored by winning two games in succession.

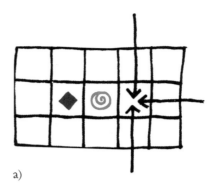

a)

Capturing

All pieces, except the King, are captured in the same way, which is by being flanked or bracketed by two enemy pieces along any row or column (example a). More than one enemy can be taken with a single move if it creates more than one 'bracket'(example b). You may safely enter the space between two enemy pieces already in place.

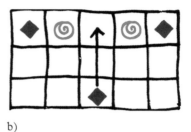

b)

Black squares count as friendly pieces to both sides when making captures (i.e. if your move brackets an enemy between yourself and a black square, you take him, see example c). The exception is the centre square when occupied by the King: it is then friendly only to White.

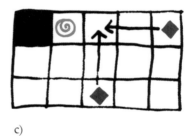

c)

The King is captured by being flanked on all four sides. Or on three sides when next to an edge or the central square (see example e). Or just two sides when on the edge and next to a corner square (example d).

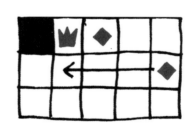

d)

a) White is captured when Red enters this space.

b) Two White pieces are captured when Red enters this space.

c) White or Red pieces can be captured by a single enemy when next to a black square.

d) King captured by two Reds when next to a corner square.

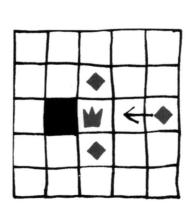

e) King captured by three Reds when next to a central square, or on an edge.

e)